HOME IS FORWARD

HIKING AND TRAVEL ADVENTURES FROM AROUND THE WORLD

ALSO BY GARY SIZER

Where's the Next Shelter?

Home is Forward

Gary Sizer

Copyright © 2017 Gary Sizer

All rights reserved. No part of this book may be reproduced, stored in a retrieval system, or transmitted in any form, or by any means, electronic, mechanical, photocopying, recording or otherwise, except for the use of brief quotations in a book review, without prior permission of the author.

Cover Illustration and Design by Mark Calcagni

Editing by Mark Houser

ISBN-13: 978-1544005386
ISBN-10: 1544005385

This book is for my mom.
She taught me to walk, and then let me go.

CONTENTS

1. Wind Up 1
2. Mail Call 8
3. The Spirit of the Woods 14
4. Possum Junction 24
5. Laughing Totem 32
6. The Land that Time Forgot 40
7. Reset 46
8. Cloud City 55
9. Day of the Condor 68
10. Temple of the Sun 83
11. Home is Forward 97
12. Dead Reckoning 115
13. Puddle Jumping 126
14. The Middle Barrens: Destroyer of Plans . 135
15. The Big Lonely 145
16. Northern Lights 154
17. Fancy Pants 161
18. The Cliffs of Woo 172
19. Light Speed 185
20. Shakedown 201

The little blond boy crouched behind a chair in the hospital waiting room and vroomed his toy motorcycle through the air along a road only he could see. Excited engine sounds, along with a little spit, sprayed from his lips as the riderless bike made lazy figure eights before him. No adult shushed him. At 3 a.m. there was no one in the waiting room to be bothered by his vrooming.

In a few minutes, a nurse would notice the empty bed, find the boy, and deposit him back into it. No alarm, no lockdown, and no media attention. This was 1972, and little boys with the flu climbed out of their hospital beds all the time without causing a collective freakout.

The collective freakout would come after the boy made his tenth escape, wriggling out of his harness and slipping through a gap in the net stretched over his crib.

That little boy was me.

CHAPTER 1
WIND UP

"S IR! R ECRUIT S IZER requests permission to speak, sir!" I sprayed a little spit when I yelled this, and some of his spit landed on me when the drill instructor barked his reply.

"Speak."

"Sir! Recruit Sizer requests permission to venture beyond the treeline in order to secure a field-expedient means by which to square away his hooch, sir!"

Marines talk funny, and in boot camp they talk funnier, but even this was too much for the DI. "God damn it, Sizer, use English."

"Sir, I need to—"

He thundered. "ARE WE ON A DATE NOW? WHY ARE YOU WHISPERING AT ME, BOY?!?"

One of the less enjoyable aspects of life on Parris Island is all the constant yelling. From the moment you step off the bus until the day you graduate, it never stops. Anyone who's ever seen a movie about Marine Corps boot camp already knows that the drill instructors do a lot of yelling. One significant aspect the filmmakers fail to show is that the recruits do a lot of yelling too. It's required.

Unless you request permission "to speak in a normal conversational tone, sir!" every word that comes out of your nasty little piehole must be shouted at top volume, or there will be hell to pay. Part of the reason for this is that it ruins your vocal cords, and eventually strengthens them when they recover, giving you the ability to project that loud, intimidating gravelly command presence associated with the jarheads. The ability to articulate while shouting also comes in handy outdoors, especially when you need to give orders as things are exploding around you. Also, when you scream everything you say, there's little room for "ums" and "ahs." A few weeks of this yields an unexpected side effect of making you confident to the extreme.

I was still far from this stage, and was momentarily distracted by the mental image of being on a date with my DI.

"SPIT IT OUT, SON!"

"Sir! I'd like to find something I can use to fix my tent!"

"Go."

He must have been tired, or my request would have been denied and I would have been thrashed for using the personal pronouns. On top of all the yelling, we always had to refer to ourselves in the third person. Looking back, I can now see the logic behind that rule. If you're trying to create a platoon of unblinking killers who instantly follow every order without question, you can't have their heads cluttered up with distracting concepts like "I" or "my."

"Aye-aye, sir!" I executed my best about-face and ran to my task. We weren't allowed to walk.

■   ■   ■

I was 21, and had only slept in a tent two other times, both here at Parris Island. But during my teenage years, I slept outside almost every night. We'd lived in a few places, mostly small apartments near Pittsburgh, so "outside" meant the porch. I could see Orion rise from the spot where I put my sleeping bag, and I loved the wind on my face at night. Still do.

Before I turned in each night, I would wander the neighborhood, sometimes alone, but often in the company of friends. A small group of similarly bored teenagers would gather at someone's house and we'd roam for hours. The internet hadn't been invented yet, and our little suburb was quiet and devoid of the one thing every teen craves most: *something to do.* So we walked. A lot.

We didn't always have a car growing up, so I also put in many miles schlepping back and forth to school, grandma's house, and to go get groceries, which I helped pay for using money from my paper route, which of course, I walked. I should have seen it coming.

The first time the Marines put a pack on me and forced me to march was the first time I really relaxed. While everyone else was limping along with blisters or hunched under the weight of their loads, I was lost in my thoughts. My pack and rifle were lighter than the bass drum I carried in marching band, so my back didn't hurt. My feet were already conditioned from years of being too poor to drive, and it was easy to drift off into a trance when the only thing you had to remember to do was occasionally say, "I don't know, but I've been told / Eskimo women are mighty cold…"

Another distinct advantage I enjoyed in boot camp was my height. Our marching formations were arranged from tallest to shortest, and as one of the lankiest recruits in the platoon I got to take a spot up front. When we were on the move, I could stare at the horizon instead of the backs of identical shaved heads.

We were also paired by height for activities, which meant that my lunch buddy, tentmate, and hand-to-hand combat partner were all the same guy, Recruit Nickles. Nickles was also six-foot-three, but he had played football, had won his local "tough guy" competition, and carried about fifty more pounds of muscle than I did. The first time we shared a tent, I squeezed into my side and did my best to lie still while he snored and sweat beside me. Eventually he'd settle, and the wind and the crickets would be my lullaby. I didn't realize it, but I was happy.

The tents we carried were of an interesting design. Each recruit is issued half of a tent, officially called a "shelter half." You get one tent pole, a few metal stakes, and enough heavy canvas to form 50 percent of a pup tent. Each shelter half has snaps that join it with any other half, so that theoretically any two random recruits can pair up and spend the night.

We had dumped our packs, and as the DIs swarmed

around us screaming orders and punishing the slowpokes, Nickles had stepped on my tent pole, snapping it in two. This is why I found myself rummaging through the brush trying to find a straight piece of pine of just the right length.

"HURRY UP! We. Are. Waiting. ON YOU, SIZER! ANY DAY NOW!"

I grabbed something too long and sprinted back, figuring I could just snap off the excess length. Nickles was standing at attention before the failed pile of canvas that was our home. The other recruits were at attention too, and had been that way the whole time—tensed up, heels together, feet at a 45-degree angle, fingers curled, thumbs at the trouser seams, head and eyes to the front, mouths shut. None of them had seen me running around, but they had all just heard my name enough times to know that any ensuing trouble would be my fault, even if it wasn't.

The DI ordered Nickles and me to "unfuck yourselves," and while we fixed our shelter, he explained what was up next. We were going to compete against another platoon in something called pugil sticks. "Pugil" is short for pugilist, which meant we were in for some good old fashioned face smashing. If you've ever seen *American Gladiators* or a similar TV show, you're familiar with the event in which two opponents square off on a balance beam, each armed with a giant padded Q-tip which they use to bash each other while wearing football helmets.

Our senior drill instructor stepped forward to motivate us. While two of his equally intimidating assistants flanked him, he explained that our victory was certain. Our success was guaranteed because the senior DI had a trick up his sleeve. An incentive which would whip us into a frenzy. Each timid recruit would be transformed into a raging berserker, because if we won, we would get an amazing reward. He told us that if we emerged victorious, he would not skin us alive and make flowerpots from our skulls. This seemed fair.

He then offered an additional incentive. A bonus so ridiculous, I took it as exaggeration (he really seemed serious about the flowerpot thing). Anyone who could hit someone from the opposing team hard enough to send them to sickbay, would get...*a phone call home!*

We lined up and marched another mile or so to the makeshift combat arena.

Again, most everything is ordered by height, so I was up first. I was pitted against someone as tall but built more like my tentmate. He was a wall of camouflage with a helmet and a stick, and he didn't look to be anywhere near as nervous as I was. As the referee lifted the whistle to his mouth, I imagined my opponent's stick flying up to my face. I could see myself toppling off the beam and into a world of pain and pushups. I was going to lose and I knew it.

The ref drew his breath and in that moment I had an idea. It was a long shot, but I knew I was outmatched physically. My opponent knew it too, and locked eyes with me.

Just as the ref blew the whistle, I blew my opponent a kiss.

He blinked and cocked his head. I heard him

mumble, "Huh?" and watched him hesitate just long enough for me to reach up and score a point by touching his chin with my stick.

Both platoons threw up their arms and booed. The senior DI was livid. "DAMN IT, SIZER, TAKE OFF THAT GEAR AND GIVE IT TO A REAL MAN! NICKLES! KILL SOMEONE!"

I took a seat, as well as a few more insults, and gave my helmet and stick to Recruit Nickles. His opponent was another tall guy, but skinny like me. "Why couldn't I get that one?" I wondered.

Before the ref had time to blow the whistle, Nickles charged across the beam, bellowing his war cry. The slender recruit didn't even have a chance to lift his stick before Nickles wound up and brained him like a silverback gorilla hitting a tee-ball. The kid was out cold instantly, flat on his back, both eyes closed. The blow knocked his helmet off, and after it rolled to a stop, someone verified that he was breathing. The kid was still unconscious when the medics hauled him off, and the next day we learned that one of the vertebrae in his neck had been cracked. He'd recover, but his military career was over before it began.

The senior DI congratulated Nickles and gave him a free pass to the pay phones. He then ordered the rest of us to give Nickles our home phone numbers so that a real man could chat up our moms while the rest of us miserable shit stains stayed back to scrub the squad bay and think about how we'd failed our country.

CHAPTER 2
MAIL CALL

LIFE IN THE SQUAD BAY was chaotic by design. That's basically the whole point of boot camp. They teach you a few things, but for the most part, the environment exists to numb you to the insanity and stresses of combat and to weed out those who crack. If you cry from being yelled at, you're probably not going to make it when the bullets start flying.

A big part of that chaos and insanity is never knowing when a drill instructor might randomly appear and start screaming. Just like in the movies, the senior DI would march up and down the center of the squad bay, angrily lecturing us about discipline or ranting on military history. His feet would strike the deck as he berated us, heels tick-tocking to mark the passage of time between physical punishments.

We stood shoulder to shoulder at attention while his assistant DIs lurked between the bunks. In my peripheral vision, their pointed hats made them look like sharks. They glided among us, silently scanning for imperfections, sniffing for a hint of blood in the water.

Any movement at all and you were the next meal. The position of attention is sacred among Marines. No one can stand perfectly still like we do. If you find yourself in a situation where you need someone to look straight ahead without blinking or moving for a really long time, call the Marines.

Actually, blinking was allowed, but that was about it. Look left or right without permission—or heaven forbid, scratch an itch—and instantly, three beasts with veiny necks are screaming in your ears while you rapidly cycle through pushups, jumping jacks, running in place and more pushups until your arms and legs stop working. That's called a "thrashing."

I made this mistake on the very first day. I didn't think anyone would see me scratch my ear, and before I even reached it there was a DI on me. He seemed to have an important question. So important that he screamed it into my ear. "WHAT IS THE MAXIMUM EFFECTIVE RANGE OF THE M-249 SQUAD AUTOMATIC WEAPON?!?"

I thought, *I don't know. I just got here, I don't even know what one of those is.* I decided to guess and said, "Twelve…parsecs?"

An instant later, another popped out from between the bunks. He pushed Nickles aside and screamed into my other ear. This one had an essay question. "RECITE YOUR ENTIRE CHAIN OF COMMAND STARTING WITH YOURSELF AND NAMING EVERYONE ALL THE WAY UP TO THE COMMANDER IN CHIEF!!!"

I wanted to say, "You?" but clammed up instead. A third DI had appeared. This one was a little guy, barely five feet tall. He was bouncing back and forth from one foot to the other, looking up at me from under the brim of his pointed hat, chanting, "You better answer him, boy! You better answer him, boy! You better answer him, boy...!"

It was too much. The only way out was down, so I dropped to the deck and just did pushups until someone else drew their ire.

Getting mail from home is equally confusing. The senior DI will sit at his desk near the front of the squad bay and call out names. That recruit must stop whatever he's doing and sprint to the DI, where he then snaps into the position of attention and hollers, "Sir! Recruit Jones reporting for mail call, sir!"

The DI then holds out the letter, which the recruit has to retrieve by swiftly and forcefully clapping his hands together on either side of the envelope, snatching it out of the DI's hands. (Do not touch the DI. That's a thrashing.) The next line in this absurd play is, "Sir! Mail received, sir!" followed by the recruit executing a perfect about-face and sprinting back to his footlocker. This is especially entertaining if the recruit has been shining his boots and has to perform the routine in slippery socks. Luckily, I had my boots on when they called my name.

"Sizer. Front and center."

I bolted to the front, clicked my heels and delivered my line. Or at least tried to. "Sir! Recruit Sizer reporting for—"

"Shut up." I did.

The senior DI was holding what appeared to be a postcard, while his three assistants leered over his shoulders, their arms crossed and jaws clenched. He glared at me from below his wide brim and thrust the card at me, holding it an inch from my eyes. "EXPLAIN!"

I leaned back and focused. Shit, I thought. Cornball Train.

Cornball Train was the nickname of my childhood friend. We've known each other since we were about 10, and for reasons neither of us can recall, whenever we're together he goes by that absurd moniker, while I am Game Show Host. My good friend Cornball Train was always an excellent student, so while I was busy scrubbing latrines at Parris Island, he was off studying Russian for the summer in the former Soviet Union. Which had to explain why my senior drill instructor was menacing me with a postcard apparently sent from Red Square.

I started to speak and he flipped it around. "EXPLAIN!"

Most of it was written in basic Russian—which I could actually read, having studied it a bit back in college, but which frustrated the drill instructors. But the true source of their outrage were the few lines my friend had written in English.

Dear Drill Sergeants...

Drill instructors hate to be called drill sergeants. (What is this, the Army?) This was the first drop of blood in the water. It continued.

There are three things you should know about my friend, Gary.

Oh no.

> 1. His arms are very weak.

Great. More blood.

> 2. He hates to do pushups.

Okay, that's fair.

> 3. He thinks he's funny.

Not anymore I don't.

He signed it:

> Love, Comrade Cornball Train

Oh god, no.

The feeding frenzy began. As soon as I finished reading, the largest of the DIs leapt over the senior's desk and began screaming in my left ear. The brim of his pointed hat pressed into my temple, forcing my head to tilt as his voice exploded. "WHAT KIND OF A NAME FOR A MARINE IS 'GARY'?!?"

I lacked an immediate response, not that I would have been able to give it. Less than a second later, his equally large and loud partner was in my other ear. My head was now pinched between the brims of their smokies; they were practically holding me up at this point. This one had another essay question prepared. "WHY ARE YOU RECEIVING ENCRYPTED CORRESPONDENCE FROM A FOREIGN AGENT BEHIND ENEMY LINES?!?"

Whoa, hang on a second, I thought. Cornball Train isn't a foreign agent. He's my friend. Or at least I thought he was. What kind of a friend does this? I had no answers.

The short DI scrambled around the desk and glared up at me like a pit bull on a chain. He rocked on his heels and chanted, "This better be funny, boy! This better be funny, boy! This better be funny, boy...!"

They all continued to barrage me while the senior demanded to know who this person was.

The sharks had me. There was no way out. "Sir!" I stammered. "He's just a friend I grew up with. Playing a joke. He's just... *(this better be funny, boy)* ...just an old chum!"

They took the bait and tore me to pieces. The pun was lost on them, but at least I enjoyed a small private giggle as I hit the deck. I did pushups until my arms failed. I ran in place and did jumping jacks until my lungs and legs defied me. I fell to my back and touched my nose to my knees until my stomach muscles burned. Then they took me outside and made me roll in sand while singing the Marine's Hymn.

My chum. Hah!

This is when I knew I would make it. They had no idea that while they were breaking my body, I was cracking up on the inside.

CHAPTER 3
THE SPIRIT OF THE WOODS

I DIDN'T EVEN KNOW I wanted to be a Marine until just a few months before boot camp. I was a junior in my first attempt at a college degree when I fell in with a crowd of rowdy art majors. I had started out in the honors program as a freshman, studying math and science. But after a few semesters with my newfound friends, I was squinting at my professors and posing what I considered to be deep questions: "Yeah, but what really *are* numbers, man?"

That summer back home after dropping all of my classes, I had a series of productive meetings with a rather persuasive Marine recruiter who also happened to be my brother. Jim had been one of the "bad kids" when we were teens. He smoked cigarettes and worked on cars instead of studying. He had cool stories about jumping fences and running from cops. I recall being amazed at the transformation boot camp had had on him. He was suddenly doing really bizarre things like getting up early, and being polite.

He convinced me that my newfound career as a line

cook was a fast track to nowhere and that I should do what he did. My own flawed rationale was that if the Marines could transform a little turd like Jim into something respectable, surely they could do nothing but good given me to work with.

When boot camp was over, I was just glad to be alive.

Recruiters—especially the ones you didn't give wet willies to when you were kids—love to talk about boot camp. Recruits sometimes forget they still have four more years to go after earning their first stripe. Jim did a good job of preparing me, though, so when I received orders to Marine Combat Training at Camp Lejeune in North Carolina, I was not surprised.

Every Marine is a rifleman. They tell you that from day one, and never let you forget it. Whether you drive a tank or push a broom, every single Marine is trained in marksmanship, land navigation, and tactics. Even if you work in an office, you still need to know how to score a head shot from a hundred yards. MCT is where they send all the new guys to learn this stuff.

When I checked in, I was still a little gung ho, excited to learn some new skills. I had done well with the rifle at Parris Island, and the promise of new, longer range weapons intrigued me. I was also very much looking forward to the map and compass work. Apparently I have a thing for activities that involve precision and accuracy at a distance, like orienteering and, as I would learn later, astronomy. (Eventually I would go on to teach orienteering to future officers.)

But on my first night patrol, despite finding my

objective and returning successfully, I would wander farther than I'd ever been in my life. And it would happen without traveling a single step.

■　■　■

"Night patrol" sounds a lot more exciting than it really is. A squad of about a dozen Marines is given an objective, some distant feature like a nondescript hilltop or a river crossing. The goal is to travel to the objective, make observations, and return with data. If something gets in your way, deal with it.

The objective might be a few hundred meters away, or it could be miles. You don't know until you get your orders. When my squad received ours, there was a twist: Once we got to our objective, we were to dig in and set an ambush against a rival squad, who thought they were doing a simple "out and back."

An extra twist was that we had no idea when our targets would arrive. When the "enemy" finally showed up, we would all point our empty weapons at one another, yell "Bang! Bang!" and either fall down or follow up with "Missed me!" It was stressful, but it was also occasionally fun.

The instructors were all experienced Marines who only barely outranked us, and lived off-base with their families. There was no way this little game of cops 'n robbers in the woods would go past ten. Midnight at the latest.

We left camp at dusk. The objective was a ridge overlooking a road roughly a mile north of our position.

What makes a patrol different than a forced march is that you maintain a constant state of tactical readiness while on the move. That meant no talking, safety switches off, and trigger fingers ready. We spread out and communicated silently, using a set of hand and arm signals that we had only just learned that afternoon.

When dusk turned to dark, we barely noticed. No flashlights are allowed on a patrol, but we didn't need them. Our eyes naturally adapt to gloom, and a waning crescent moon shone down upon us. Nevertheless, it was still slow going. A mile takes a while when you're trying to be stealthy.

Our platoon commander was with us, a fresh lieutenant who was also being trained. An instructor tailed us silently, taking notes.

When I located the ridge, the young officer beckoned me over. I jogged to his position and whispered, "Sir, Private Sizer reporting as ordered, sir." I almost saluted him, but then I remembered. Snipers. If there are any snipers about, the first bullet typically hits any person on the receiving end of a salute. Target number two is usually the guy with the antenna, and once you lose those two, you're toast. Granted, our biggest actual threat would be someone from the opposing squad yelling, "Bang bang!" at our CO, but I'm pretty sure that dish came with a side order of pushups.

"Sizer, do you know how to set an ambush?"

I did, at least in theory. Our instructor had drawn one on the board during class and I demonstrated by drawing one in the dirt. "We're here." I placed a rock, and dragged my finger to create a shallow groove.

"That's the road. We post two guards here and here while we dig in. If they retreat..." I tried to seem thoughtful. "They'll get stuck...here." I was making it all up as I went.

"Looks good, private. Make it happen."

"Aye, sir." I jogged back to the squad and told them what they already knew. Spread out, find a place to hide, point your rifles that way, and wait.

Our first attempt at digging in was not a success. We were too close together. The instructor chastised me. "If you want to kill yourself, fine. But don't get so close to your buddy that the same grenade takes out both of you. It's disrespectful." He explained that each of us should just barely be able to see the Marine to our left and right.

We all adjusted, and by the time we'd piled rocks and leaves around our individual positions the moon had sunk noticeably. I worked out that it must be about nine o'clock or so, which meant that our victims should be here any minute now.

▪ ▪ ▪

Once everyone finally stopped rustling and fidgeting, I could hear the crickets. They were the only sound except for the occasional sniff or scratch. Eventually those noises ceased as well, especially after our instructor descended upon my neighbor, berating him in a stage whisper for getting us all killed, thanks to his lack of discipline.

I stuck my elbows in the dirt and stared down the barrel of my rifle. Any minute now. The moon was behind us. Good, I thought. It'll light 'em up like a spotlight.

It was August, so the air was warm and still. When the moon ultimately dropped below the horizon, the ensuing blackness was the signal for the crickets to stop. Now the only sound was my breathing. In the dead calm of that pitch dark night, it was the loudest noise in the world. With every breath, I thought, *they can hear me.*

I slowed my breath, still hearing it and nothing else. With no basis for comparison, I had no idea how loud I actually was, and obsessing over it was going to drive me nuts. I closed my eyes.

Bad idea, Gary, I thought. The temptation to sleep was immediate and overwhelming, but snoozing at the trigger was an actual crime, one that carried a penalty far worse than a thrashing.

I raised my head and scanned left, then right, looking for the human-shaped piles of leaves and rocks that were my nearest neighbors. Without the moon, all the surrounding lumps looked the same. That rock might be a person or vice versa. I had no way to tell.

My elbows began to ache, but I knew from weeks on the rifle range that it would pass. Soon they would go numb, and shortly after that, the fingers on my non-trigger hand. I opened and closed them slowly. Already tingling. Any minute now.

That minute passed, or maybe it was an hour. Any hint of the moon's glow was long gone, and now the stars were beginning to twinkle through the trees. The leaves were too thick for me to pick out any constellations, so the effect was disorienting. I began to feel dizzy. The world wasn't spinning; I was.

I picked a star and locked onto it. The spinning stopped, but now I could detect a low humming sound. I blinked once, then twice, and then opened my eyes as wide as I could. That didn't help me hear any better, although I could swear the hum was getting louder.

I shook my head and focused on my star again. For a moment, I forgot I was a Marine on his belly in the dirt and simply existed as a pair of eyes soaking in the starlight. That light was amazing, really. The more I thought of it, the more incredible the idea became. That dim shine, not even close to casting a shadow, was coming from a thing bigger than the sun, and *millions of miles away*. Then I also remembered that it had taken millions of years for that light to reach me. Those photons had traveled *across the universe* for me. They even had to avoid the leaves on that tree. Why, if I had been a foot to the left, I never would have seen it.

I blinked without blinking and the hum became a voice. Someone was humming the letter M in a deep baritone, relentlessly, calmly, and without ever pausing for breath. *It's a machine come to life*, I thought, and then floated free from my body.

I was only a few feet up, but I could see myself clearly. I was in the prone position with my rifle pointed in the right direction, but my eyes were wide and my jaw was slack. I saw myself take a silent breath and heard me think, *any minute now.*

The humming voice said, "Gary" and I floated higher. I could see the rest of my squad. One of them was asleep, and another had wet himself rather than make noise by getting up.

The other squad wasn't coming.

The voice hummed my name again and I floated back down into my body. I blinked for real this time and found myself briefly looking out from behind my actual eyes. They could see nothing. I couldn't feel my hands, so I waved the idea of one in front of my face, but it was lost too. Nothing.

Nothing to see, nothing to feel, the humming voice became everything. Since there was only the voice, I listened, but not with my ears. "Look," it said.

I looked without my eyes and saw a tree. It was a sprawling oak, the oldest of trees. Its branches were a million craggy arms, each with a million green hands, its bark was made of flowery eyes. "You are safe here," it said in a booming green hum.

"Where am I?" I asked.

"You are here, now."

Of course. I knew this. I felt a strong sense of peace, bordering on euphoria. "And, are you…?"

"Yes," the voice hummed. "We are the Spirit of the Woods." Every eye on the ancient oak turned to me, observing but not judging. Caring, but not loving. Insisting. "Listen."

"Yes," I said and listened, without my ears.

Wordlessly the eyes spoke their message. They told me silently that everything was connected. Every particle in the universe was simply energy condensed to a point, and that all of those points made the stuff which powers the stars. The Spirit of the Woods told me that everything is made of light, that when the stars die they fling their remains into the void, and that all of that cosmic flotsam and jetsam becomes us, but that "us" wasn't the right word because it implied separation. All of the vibrating energy in the universe is the only thing that is. We are constructed of the same stuff, just stacked differently. It told me that I was the trees and the trees were me, and that when you shoot the enemy, you are only shooting yourself.

My cheeks were wet. I touched one and before I knew what to wonder next, I heard a loud *SNAP!* I was back on the ridge, my real eyes were open and there was definitely someone behind me.

"Sizer!" It was our instructor. He had just stepped on a twig. "On your feet."

I had difficulty standing, as both my legs had fallen asleep. I almost dropped my rifle and wobbled a bit once I was up. "Yes, sir?"

"HQ radioed. Those other dipshits got lost. Pack it up. Looks like you boys will be getting some sleep tonight after all."

He disappeared into the brush and I checked my watch. We had been there for ten hours.

■ ■ ■

Almost every culture has its own version of "forty days and forty nights," where some young person is sent into the wilderness to survive, or to have a vision, or both. It's a rite of passage, a way to select or strengthen the tribe's warriors. The individual is stripped of everything. No clothes, no weapons, no food. The ones that come back are transformed in a way that the elders recognize and the uninitiated envy. The calm confidence in one's own abilities coupled with a dash of enlightenment is a powerful combination. But what does a modern warrior do with that?

I spent ten hours accidentally meditating on a ridge. This came after months of starving, hardly sleeping and joining in group chants. I shaved my head. I'm not sure whether any of that adds up to a vision quest or not, but I definitely felt different after that experience, in a way that's taken me years to process. I'm still not sure I fully understand.

It had been dark, completely silent and the perfect temperature with no breeze. That ridge was nothing more than a natural sensory deprivation chamber. I recognize that my mind was desperately craving input of any kind, so it began creating its own. And yet... There's this nagging sense of something I can't quite put my finger on. The persistent notion of *I know what I saw.*

I often wonder how many other modern soldiers have heard from the Spirit of the Woods, and what they learned. I know that sometimes I can still call upon it by simply going on a hike. I'll find a log or a rock and just sit and wait until I feel something call to me. It says, *"You are here, now. Safe."*

CHAPTER 4
POSSUM JUNCTION

OVER THE NEXT few years, I performed a number of unusual duties, none of which I even knew were jobs that Marines needed to do. After combat training, they sent me to a three-week class where I learned how to stack crates in the cargo hold of a ship. After those three weeks, I never stacked another crate.

Instead, my first duty station after training was Okinawa, where I worked in the general's building. Someone caught wind of the fact that I could type, so I was assigned to a vault full of secret folders. My job was to find the right folder and read the correct number to someone who knew what it meant. I found the daily aromas of coffee and shoe polish to be more pleasant than mud and gunpowder, but each day in the vault I missed trees.

After a year of that, I was sent to Quantico, where I had the unique responsibility of teaching new lieutenants two things: how to find distant objectives in the dark, and which fork to use during the salad course. There had been budget cuts, and using a land navigation expert to also teach social etiquette only made sense. For a brief period, I had a government-issued custom tailored tuxedo and a whole storage room full of silver candelabras. (If you're wondering how such things were possible during those lean fiscal times, they were Vietnam-era silver candelabras, sorely in need of replacement.)

So far, I had experienced virtually nothing that my recruiter promised. Just when I thought I might finally get to ride in a helicopter or blow something up, Uncle Sam sent me to the Naval ROTC unit at the University of Missouri. Among other things, I was charged with training midshipmen, turning young men and women into leaders, and molding the craziest among them into Marines. I often found myself in hot water for being too polite. What did they expect? I just spent the previous two years gently encouraging young officers to "go ahead and lift that pinky when you drink. It's classy, sir!"

By some miracle, I was able to use my time on campus to finish my degree. By some other miracle, perhaps aided by the fact that I marched around campus in dress blues, I found a girlfriend. She had been in the program briefly; Katie was training to be a fighter pilot. When she broke her ankle during a nasty rappelling accident, they booted her out of ROTC and into my heart. Things were just starting to get serious when it was time for me to go again.

Someone at headquarters had caught wind that I had taken and passed this three-week-long box stacking course seven years ago, and that I, as a newly pinned sergeant would be the perfect person to put in charge of deploying a real live infantry battalion at Camp Lejeune, complete with tanks, planes, a couple thousand troops, and all their gear. The job starts next week, best of luck.

■ ■ ■

When I reported for duty again at Camp Lejeune, I met with the battalion sergeant major and attempted the opposite of a job interview. I needed to warn the man in charge that I was wrong for the job. He wasn't having it.

"You are a sergeant, correct?"

"Yes, sergeant major." I was at attention, staring at a point behind his head.

"And I see here in your record book that you are a successful graduate of 0431 Embarkation and Logistics School, correct?"

That three-week-long box stacking class from seven years ago. If I could have sighed, I would have. "Yes, Sergeant Major."

He slapped a folder onto his desk and stood. "And these are your orders to report to me as the new embark chief, correct?"

"Correct, sergeant major."

"So what is there to discuss?"

I requested permission to speak freely and summarized my career. He found the part about the candelabras to be significant. Apparently because I had to put them away neatly after each dinner, I was now qualified to load cargo onto a ship. It was basically the same thing. Now get the hell out of my office, you sandbagging piece of lint.

For the first time since joining up, I was unhappy. The work was uninteresting and I was terrible at it, which meant I was perpetually in trouble. Even worse, so was my unit. With me in charge, we were never going to get anywhere. There are rooms full of binders full of rules about what's allowed to be stacked next to what. The sergeant major considered sending me to advanced training, but the classes lasted longer than the time I had left on my final tour and I was not reenlisting.

The command's distaste for me was a constant source of misery, and my only relief was my long distance relationship with Katie, the young lady with the bad ankle. She was still back in Missouri with one more year left before graduating.

. . .

We hadn't seen each other in months when the sergeant major displayed a rare moment of kindness. Independence Day was coming up, and he was giving us a "ninety-six"—a four-day pass, usually granted to coincide with a holiday. It's free time off and not counted as leave, a service member's official vacation time. The only stipulation is that you have to stay within a 700-mile radius of the base, just in case we have to scramble.

Columbia, Mo., is just over a thousand miles away.

Too bad, I thought. I'm going anyway.

This was a terrible idea for many reasons. Going out of bounds was a serious offense. Not making it back in time, according to the Uniform Code of Military Justice, was a crime called "unauthorized absence," and the punishment was brig time.

The trip would take 20 hours each way, assuming I didn't stop. That's a long haul. I did not want to meet the Spirit of the Highway. So I drank coffee and smoked cigars the whole way. I sped with the windows down and plugged my portable CD player into the cassette deck of my 15-year-old hatchback with one hubcap and sang my heart out to stay awake. *Here they come to snuff the rooster, oh yeah.*

The thrill I felt from being out of bounds and on my own was enough to keep me alert the whole way. Less than 24 hours later, stinking and jittery, I fell into bed with the girl of my dreams. Our time together was so special that I seriously considered just hunkering down and changing my name or growing a mustache. I can't do either of those things, so when it was time to go, 24 hours before roll call a thousand miles away, I accepted my fate and kissed her goodbye.

■ ■ ■

The return trip was a rush. Again, staying awake was going to be a challenge, but even worse, I was going to arrive with just enough time to take a shower and report in for a full day's work. I didn't care. I was still riding the high from my secret romantic getaway.

My CD collection was getting stale, so somewhere in the middle of Indiana, I switched to the books-on-tape edition of Stephen Hawking's *A Brief History of Time*. The narrator was right in the middle of reminding me that everything in the universe is connected when the engine stopped making the car go.

There was no bang, no satisfying thud, just the slow whine of the motor giving out. I stepped on the gas, saw the tach rev up, but my speed continued to drop. I checked that I wasn't in neutral, and when I looked back up, the road was obscured by a thick veil of white smoke billowing from under the hood. I checked my mirror, and no one was tailing me. I drifted into the breakdown lane, fell out the door and scrambled away to cough and spit. I'd blown a radiator hose before and that was definitely not steam I was inhaling.

I stood and surveyed the damage. The smoke had mostly cleared, and now I could detect liquid pooling beneath the car. Oil and antifreeze mixed in a grungy puddle, and upon closer examination, why yes, that was steam mixed in with the smoke too. Apparently every system had failed catastrophically and simultaneously.

Well, Sergeant Sizer, looks like you need a plan, I thought.

It was 1998, which is important to mention because in that year only millionaires had cell phones. I had an atlas, my wallet, and a sack full of laundry, and that was it. That and half a cigar.

I looked back and saw corn. Ahead, left, and right, more of the same. I was hoping for a road sign so I could at least estimate where I was. I had been daydreaming and couldn't remember what exit I had passed last, or even how long ago. Without that information, I was stuck.

I walked a lap around the car. That accomplished

nothing, but made me feel better for a second.

It was 3 p.m., and 6 a.m. was 15 hours away. Even if I got this thing running right now I'd still just barely make it. Who could I call, and how? And even if I could reach someone, what would I say? "Hi, Gary here. Could you let the sergeant major know I'll be late tomorrow? I'm stuck in some corn." Shit. I'm a dead man.

I fell to my knees, swearing and shaking my fist at the sky, then burying my face in my hands. A gray sedan rolled to a stop just behind my smoking hulk. The driver's window lowered and a young lady with skin the color of chocolate leaned out and smiled. "Are you okay?"

I looked at myself and then my car. "I am, thanks. This thing's not."

"Anything I can do to help?"

What are the odds, I thought. "Uh…only if you're on your way to North Carolina."

She laughed.

"Yeah, that's what I thought."

"Camp Lejeune?" she asked. That got my attention.

"Actually, yes. How—" she pointed to the center of her windshield. It bore the tiny sticker required by the Defense Department for vehicles to enter a military base.

"I'm going near there. You coming back from the ninety-six?"

I was, and so was she. She was a sergeant in the Army, on her way back to Fort Bragg, just short of my destination. It was a sure spot better than this cornfield, and if it came down to it, calling in late from there would at least put me back within bounds, possibly halving my sentence.

"What do you want to do about your car?"

That was a good question. I couldn't just leave it there. Or could I? "I don't know. Where are we?"

"There's a town called Bristow a few miles ahead. Want to see if someone there can tow it? Maybe you can come back in a few weeks and get it."

Yeah, I thought. They can tow it all right. I grabbed my bag, took the registration from the console and joined my new friend. When we reached the next exit we followed the signs to a little country store called Possum Junction. I found someone with a tow truck, and when he told me how much it would cost to bring it in, I handed him the registration.

"You trying to sell me a car, son?"

"No sir, I'm giving it to you." I told him where to find it, and added that he might be able to get fifty dollars for the tires. That should cover the cost of the tow. We shook on it, and I never saw him or that car again.

My new traveling companion and I switched off between napping and driving and reached Fort Bragg early enough that she offered to take me all the way back to my place before reporting in at her own. I never saw her again either, but I did get her address and that Christmas I sent her a very nice card.

And as for Katie, my whole reason for risking my neck? I definitely saw her again. In fact, I married her.

CHAPTER 5
LAUGHING TOTEM

THE FIRST AND ONLY time I proposed, she shot me down.

It wasn't so much the idea of marrying me that Katie was opposed to, it was the idea of being engaged. At least in the traditional sense. Long before we moved in together, it had become obvious to both of us that things were getting serious. I was sure that she was "the one," but when I hinted at picking out a ring she was quick to put the brakes on my plan: "Don't even think about it."

I was dumbfounded. What had I done wrong? She saw my expression and took my hand. "I didn't mean it like that," she said. "It's just, diamonds are dumb. We love each other, right? I know it, you know it, and that's what really matters. If you're going to blow that kind of cash to show it, at least spend it on something we can use. Like a TV or a stereo."

I guess I shouldn't have been surprised; she's always held unusual opinions on mundane matters. For instance, she staunchly opposes pierced ears. "Stabbing yourself with a needle purely for decorative purposes is dumb," is her position. That this rule doesn't apply to her tattoos is apparently not a contradiction. Katie is a strong-willed, complex woman who doesn't play by anyone's rules. Not even her own.

She really was serious about the ring thing, so instead of a cheap diamond, we split the cost of a decent television. And if we should ever be faced with enough compelling reasons to actually get married, she explained, she would not be taking on my last name. She already had a last name and it seemed like a giant pain in the ass to change it.

I didn't really care one way or the other. We agreed on plenty of other matters. Vital core beliefs, things such as the importance of spending time outdoors. With both of us freshly freed of our military obligations, we still felt the need to run and jump and swim and climb things as often as possible. We were living in western Pennsylvania. My first civilian job was fixing computers at a nuclear plant, Katie worked for an architect in Pittsburgh, and almost every weekend we found an excuse to get out.

One day after work she asked me if I'd ever want to try kayaking. In my mind's eye I pictured Eskimos throwing spears from sealskin boats.

"There's a class in a few weeks and I'd like us to go." It was up in New York, just a few hours away, designed for first-timers who wanted to get into whitewater paddling. The notion of paddling through rapids and over waterfalls had never occurred to me. She made it sound fun though, so I agreed.

We drove north and set up camp on an easy section of the Salmon River. The instructors were experienced young hotshots who dressed funny (no one looks cool in a neoprene skirt), talked weird (they used terms like "PFD" and "wet exit"), and brought a trailer full of brightly colored, surprisingly small, hard plastic boats.

The first hotshot demonstrated that whitewater kayaks aren't so much a vessel that you board, but rather more like a snug bubble, a thing that you wear. He squeezed himself into one and we each did our best to copy him.

I donned my PFD (personal flotation device, a.k.a. "life vest") and a wide-bottomed neoprene skirt that hugged my midsection very snugly. I slid into my kayak and found that, with knees slightly bent, my feet pressed all the way up against the kayak's front end. The seat offered nothing more than a few inches of lower back support. With considerable effort, I stretched the skirt around the opening. When it snapped into place, everything from my chest down was sealed in and watertight. It was like being duct taped into a plastic bathtub.

"Before we get in the water," the instructor said, "we have to practice exiting. Notice the grab loop at the front of your skirt. Give it a pull."

I grabbed and pulled. Nothing. The instructors laughed. Every single one of us was stuck.

"See? That's why we practice on dry land first. You're in there real tight. Yank hard!"

This time I pretended I was starting a lawn mower. Even with me leaning into the pull, it was still a challenge. Finally the elastic let go with a *pop!* and using both hands, I squirmed and wriggled out, falling over in the process.

"What if we have to get out while we're still in the water?" someone asked. "We'll capsize!"

"Don't worry," said our hotshot. "You'll already be upside down."

He wasn't joking either. This was called the "wet exit." We'd have to pop our skirts and push out while upside down underwater. And that was our next lesson in the river: We had to wet exit three times before they ever handed us a paddle.

It took about five minutes to perfect the wet exit. But it took about five months for me to learn to roll the boat upright using only my paddle. That particular skill is a lot like riding a bike, in that it makes no sense at all when you think about it, the first time you get it right is always by surprise, and after that as if by some magic you can do it easily, any time you like. Almost.

■ ■ ■

Over the next couple years we kayaked more and more often, and found ourselves frequenting the Southeast. Not long after, and for reasons completely unrelated to the sport, we moved to Savannah. Katie on a whim took a solo weekend trip there and fell in love with the place. "We need to live there!" she announced upon her return, then spent the next months searching for a place to live and a job in Savannah's historic district. She got a job as a bookkeeper, and I found one fixing computers, this time for a homebuilder.

Savannah is one of two Southern cities—the other is

Charleston—that were not destroyed in the Civil War in General Sherman's march to the sea. Savannah was even "gifted" to President Lincoln by the general. These two cities are the only surviving examples of Southern antebellum architecture on a grand scale.

Not only was the town beautiful and more walkable than anywhere we had been before, but we also were much closer to some of the best rivers in the country. I had come to love the river—not any particular one, but all the places on this earth that can never be accessed by car, bike, horse, or even on foot. I've drifted beneath clouds and watched great blue herons fly overhead while turtles basked on logs an arm's length away. I've seen curling foam up close, and spray on the rocks making tiny rainbows in the middle of a flowery gorge. I've sipped cider on a flat rock surrounded on all sides by rapids and waterfalls. I've swung from vines and jumped from small cliffs. I've been submerged in a few lovely spots too, both on purpose and not. And at the end of the day, my friends, a warm fire, and my tent always awaited.

Kayaking became everything, and we went every chance we got. Instead of owning proper adult furniture, we used our little apartment primarily as a place to store boats, paddles, and helmets. We watched our shared TV from lawn chairs in the living room. Sometimes I'd fold mine away and sit in my boat on the floor. I'd watch *The Simpsons* in it while rocking back and forth, increasing the extent of my lean until I could kiss the floor, pushing off and throwing my boat-clad body left, then right, strengthening the muscles I needed to properly roll on the river. Luckily our downstairs neighbor was a stumbling drunk who spent most of her evenings unconscious; otherwise she would have suspected that Katie and I led much more interesting lives than we actually did.

During the work week, I would surf BoaterTalk from the office. The online message board is where Katie and I coordinated group kayaking trips, chatted with other paddlers, read trip reports, caught up on gear reviews, and did pretty much anything other than our actual jobs. Everyone on BoaterTalk had cool-sounding names too, like Danger Judy, Psychic Midget, and Laughing Totem.

Laughing Totem was one of the site admins, and rumor had it that he was an amazing Class V paddler, a skilled rock climber, a pro photographer, and as if all that weren't enough, he was allegedly handsome to boot. I couldn't say, I'd never met the guy. I did know that he threw around a lot of Simpsons quotes on the internet, which meant he was probably okay.

. . .

Every year the folks from BoaterTalk found multiple excuses to get dozens or even hundreds of paddlers together. We would reserve entire campgrounds, sometimes spilling over into local cabin rentals. Everyone had different skill levels, so we'd break into smaller groups during the day, paddle our respective class rivers, and reassemble at night for drunken revelry around hot tubs or bonfires.

Katie and I were getting ready to test our mettle on

some intermediate rapids, and while we were dropping off some better boaters, our friend Danger Judy introduced us to Laughing Totem. Actually it wasn't so much an introduction as it was a fan boy moment. She tapped Katie on the arm and excitedly pointed him out.

"Look! There he is!"

"What do I say?" Katie asked.

Laughing Totem had just finished an early morning run on something crazy and powerful, a real whitewater chunderfest, full of big drops, holes, and boulders. He was still wearing his helmet and PFD, and from a distance looked like any other kayaker.

"How do you even know that's him?" I wondered aloud. Danger Judy said she recognized his gear, a method of identification common to boaters, skiers, hikers, snowmobile riders, and anyone who engages in activities involving brightly colored tech.

"Go ask him about his photos," she told Katie, and followed her over.

I joined them, and we found him strapping his boat to the roof of his car. I would have said hello, but he had just taken his shirt off and I was temporarily dazzled by his chiseled abs glistening in the sun, so Katie spoke up.

"Hey, you must be Laughing Totem."

He turned and smiled, offering a hand. "Mark," he said, and we switched to our real names. "Whatcha paddling today?" he asked.

I was embarrassed to say because it was something easy, but Mark wasn't the type who needed to be impressed. He seemed genuinely glad to meet us and obviously happy that we were out enjoying the water.

Katie brought up the subject of photography and Mark beamed, and offered to show us some prints in his car. They were mostly nature landscapes. One was a lone tree growing out of a rock, rendered dramatically in black and white. Another showed starry skies over high desert. The one that caught my eye was an autumn scene full of rust-colored trees against the blue misty backdrop of rolling hills.

Now that Mark's shirt was back on I found my tongue again. "Damn, dude. These are pretty amazing. I'd hang any of these in my living room!"

"How much for this one?" asked Katie, holding up the autumn scene.

Mark laughed. "Aw, you know what? I don't really know. I just got these from the printer and I forget how much they charged me. Just take it and we'll square up later."

"Are you sure? I don't think we're camping at the same place."

"Nah, don't worry about it." he insisted. "I'm sure we'll run into each other again."

CHAPTER 6
THE LAND THAT TIME FORGOT

THE FIRST AND ONLY time she proposed, I said yes.

Yet somehow, every year I still manage to forget our anniversary. I don't feel bad or offer to apologize though, because Katie also fails to recall the date. We usually remember only when Katie opens the annual card from her mother. "Oh hey!" she'll yell from the kitchen. "Apparently last week was our anniversary!"

Sometimes someone will ask us, and if we put our heads together we can talk it through and arrive at something close to the actual date. We both know it was January and it was definitely a Friday—we're just not sure which one. "We could look it up," I'll say. The documents are in the bottom of our safe, but we never go in there. It's more fun this way.

■ ■ ■

Each block in downtown Savannah is home to graceful and lovingly restored pre-Civil War mansions with brick or stone carriage houses. Live oaks sprawl overhead shading the squares, their long branches dripping with Spanish moss. Magnolias and azaleas bloom in the parks while horse drawn carriages convey wide-eyed lovers over cobblestone roads. It's the sort of place where pedestrians actually *saunter*. Replete with old Southern charm, Savannah truly is a place out of time.

We kept ourselves and our gear in a little townhouse just at the edge of the historic district. The grocery stores and parking lots have to go somewhere, and we found a place right on that line. It was in this apartment that we discovered that we could save a lot of money on health insurance if we would just go ahead and get married.

We were reading in bed one night when Katie sighed and handed me a page full of figures. "Look at these numbers," she said. "If we're going to keep doing this, we should get married." I checked her math and the plan was solid, so I agreed. We went to sleep and in the morning she called her boss to get the day off and I called mine. That's how we remember it was a Friday.

The next order of business was to find someone who had the power to make this idea into a reality. We had done zero planning, so my suggestion that we simply walk around town visiting random churches until we were no longer single seemed a half decent start.

Who knew getting married was so hard? One church required a reservation plus a huge cash deposit. Another told us we'd need at least six weeks of meetings with an elder. Even the Unitarians, the most freewheeling group of hippies to ever worship a question mark told us they couldn't spontaneously wed us.

It was getting hot, so we sauntered back home to

rethink our plan. Katie picked up the phone book and informed me, "I'll be upstairs trying to find someone who can do this on short notice. You get on the internet and see if you can download us a pre-nup."

I didn't recall discussing any kind of prenuptial agreement, probably because we'd only been engaged a few hours. But I was a team player who had been given an assignment, so I dove into my task. A few moments later, as I was printing the pages, Katie came back downstairs smiling. "Good news! I found someone to marry us!"

"That's great!" I signed the pre-nup and handed it to her along with a pen.

"I found this guy in the Yellow Pages. He's a retired Army chaplain who does beach weddings out on Tybee Island. His ad says 'tuxedos and flip-flops in the sand.' Anyhow, he's on his way downtown to drop off some papers at the courthouse, so I told him where to meet us. He said he'd do a quick ceremony for us and that's it."

"Sounds good to me." I looked around the living room. If he were coming here, we'd need to find him a place to sit. Our furniture consisted entirely of two folding chairs and some boats leaned up against the far wall.

For our wedding, Katie had selected Johnny Ganem's, a well-known Savannah landmark. It's conveniently located and everyone is familiar with it because Johnny Ganem's is the best liquor store in town.

I'm up for a lot of crazy stuff, but here I drew the line. "We're going to do this like civilized humans," I told her. "Call him back and tell him to meet us at the pub."

She did, and the chaplain agreed. Six Pence Pub would be the perfect location for our impromptu ceremony. A few short blocks from the town's most iconic park, Six Pence is a charming English-style pub. And it was only one beer away from home. Savannah is one of the few places in the United States with practically no open container restrictions, so as long as your drink is in a plastic cup, you can wander the streets with a beer in your hand. Since you can walk into any bar and order a beer to go, we measured Savannah distances in beers. River Street, for instance, was two beers away. We could leave the house with a full cup, refill at one of several reputable establishments along the way, and then revel for hours by the water. In retrospect, these loose regulations may have contributed to the foggy nature of many of my memories from this time and place.

We reached Six Pence just as we were finishing our last sips. The hostess took our empty cups and seated us at a table outside just as the chaplain arrived. He looked exactly as you would expect someone to look who makes his living performing beach weddings. He wore shorts and sandals, and his teeth blazed white in contrast to his tan scruffy face and dark wavy hair, which hung just past the collar of his Hawaiian shirt.

He took off his shades and ordered a round. After some small talk, the chaplain wanted to hear more about our plan. "So, do you guys have any vows or prepared words you want me to say?"

Katie looked at me and I shrugged. "Wow," I said.

"Um, last night she proposed with a chart. This was kind of a rush job. What do you usually recommend in this situation?"

He smiled and took a sip of beer. "You guys seem pretty cool. How about we do this?" He put his drink in the center of the table and waved his hand over it in a slow circle, while staring at us with mock seriousness. "Blah, blah, blah," he intoned. "You're official."

He then picked his glass back up and raised it, smiling as he took a swig. That was our signal to do the same. We clinked glasses and each took a sip. Then, for good measure, I gave her a kiss. After all, we were blah-blah-blah official.

"Just like that?" I said. "That's really it?"

He laughed. "Yep, that's it. We just need to sign a few things and you guys'll be the real deal."

We finished our beers and our waitress returned with champagne and cheesecake, compliments of the house. We thanked her and asked if she would be our witness. She agreed, and after we secured her signature on the appropriate line, we shared the cake and had more drinks.

The chaplain offered to take all the forms to the courthouse for us, since he was headed that way anyhow. Katie declined on the grounds that we were also eventually headed that way, after one more stop. We paid the good man for his services, gathered our things, thanked him again and left.

The one more stop we needed to make was just around the corner, at the UPS store. They had a two dollar notary public on duty, and we needed to see him because I still had the pre-nup we'd printed earlier that morning.

At the courthouse, no one seemed to notice or care that we smelled a little boozy, nor did they notice or care that we were married before we filed our pre-nup. In fact, all the officials seemed to have that same blah-blah-blah attitude. I don't think any of it mattered. Our copy of that particular document is still somewhere in the bottom of our safe. But we rarely go in there. It's more fun that way.

CHAPTER 7
RESET

ADRENALINE IS LIKE a spice. You don't need nearly as much as you think and it's easy to go overboard. It took nearly drowning for me to discover the tipping point between just enough and too much of the stuff.

One hot summer day the year Katie and I got married, we were on the Tuckasegee River with most of our BoaterTalk friends. Danger Judy, Katie and I were in our kayaks, while our pal Psychic Midget paddled with his wife in a ridiculous oversize craft called a Shredder— basically two 10-foot inflatable torpedoes made of tire rubber connected by a seating pad with barely enough room for two humans and a cooler. It's a small barge built for big water and is generally considered unflippable, unless you are really trying.

In whitewater, paddles are almost exclusively used for steering. The river water is moving so fast that you don't need to paddle, you just go. A kayak has a flat bottom with no keel, which allows it to rotate effortlessly. You simply dip a blade into the water for a second or two, creating a rudder long enough to alter your course. Skilled paddlers can make a Class V river into their own personal rollercoaster just by riding, steering, and staying upright.

The Tuckasegee is an easy river, Class II, maybe II+ in a spot or two but basically it's beginner water. For long stretches the water is perfectly flat, almost still. The boat would slow to a near halt, matching the lethargic pace of the cool water. That flat keel, designed for quick pivots, was also perfect for long lazy loops.

I leaned back, resting the paddle across my chest. With my eyes closed I could feel the sun on my face, rotating as the boat spun slowly, like a leaf on a pond. I could hear my friends laughing and splashing, occasionally interrupted by the approaching *whoosh* of a small rapid or some shoals. I'd snap to attention long enough to navigate the next obstacle and then drift back into a state of meditative bliss, watching the dragonflies land and take off from my hull.

Less than a mile from the end of the run, there's a wave train—about fifty yards of what Katie calls "the splashy parts." The water gets deep, and as it flows over the boulders below it creates stationary waves on the surface. Those waves keep rolling without moving, the opposite of what we see at the ocean, where the water stays put as the waves move.

The Tuck was one of our favorite rivers because of this wave train. If you knew what to look for, it was possible to surf some of the bigger waves. I steered my boat into a trough between two crests, spun around so that I was facing upstream, caught my wave, and played in it for a few minutes.

Surfing a kayak was a skill still relatively new to me. The water wasn't particularly fast, so I had plenty of time to react, dipping my blade first left, then right, carving a zigzag path but going nowhere, like a seagull hovering in a strong breeze.

I could hear my friends floating further downstream, and when I turned to see where they were, I overextended my balance and tipped. Instinctively, I braced. My paddle blade hit the water edge on, sliced right through the surface, and in I went.

Besides the sudden shock of cold and wet, the most unnerving thing about flipping a kayak is the sound. The white noise and hiss from the rapids above is immediately replaced by the whoosh of your ears filling with water and then silence. There's still sound down there, but you feel it more than you hear it. The splooshes and plunks of submerged rocks tumbling in the current registers in your chest rather than your ears. As you hang upside down, there's nothing to see, only green swirling and bubbles. Best to keep your eyes closed.

I was calm. I'd been inverted dozens of times, though usually it was on purpose and in still water with someone standing nearby to offer a hand. I was good at uprighting under those less intense conditions, and had even done it on the river a few times. All I had to do was lean in, position my paddle just so, and—

And nothing.

My paddle was caught in between some rocks. Trying to hold it tightly against the force of the moving water was like catching a tree branch just before hitting the ground. I felt something tear and let go, and a hot, dull ache radiated from my shoulder. My right arm would not move.

The tumbling rocks I had felt in my chest a second ago were nothing compared to what my heart was doing now. This was not at all like practice.

Wet exit. Now.

I reached for the grab loop with my left hand and pulled, but it was too tight. This was a two-handed job, not only to pop my skirt, but then to push out of the boat; I was wedged in there.

I heard a bang and my teeth clacked together as a flash of white popped behind my closed eyes. Something had smacked me in the helmet. Must have been one of the boulders under the wave train. If I was where I thought I was, the river was about to become shallow again, allowing my head and face to meet *all* the rocks.

Worse, I had gone down on an exhale, which meant I didn't have the luxury of full lungs to sort this out. The need to inhale was overwhelming.

I reached across my body to feel my right arm, and it wasn't there. It was too low, practically in my rib cage. My shoulder was out of its socket. Another rock thudded against my helmet. *I'm still going backwards.*

Near panic, I grabbed my right elbow and started twisting and wrenching the useless limb until I felt a sickening crunch, followed by a *pop* which ached all the way down to my groin.

Almost instantly, I had ten working fingers again. I could feel and use my right arm, but just barely. The pain was incredible and my chest burned. I grabbed the loop with both hands and yanked. My heart thudded and I felt another *pop*, but this time it was my skirt releasing. I pushed and wiggled, and as soon as my legs were free I began kicking and flailing. My head broke the surface and I gasped, sucking down plenty of water in the process.

I coughed and spat, looking in every direction for my friends. There they were, paddling furiously against the current to reach me, but getting nowhere, desperate seagulls fighting the gale. I could hear them yelling after me, and I offered a weak "thumbs up" before one-arm dog-paddling to the shore. There I flopped onto the pebbles, took off my helmet, and vomited river water.

Through teary eyes I watched my boat and paddle float by. My friends gathered up my flotsam before it went too far downstream (the slang for this is "a yard sale") and I walked along the bank to where they had stopped.

Katie paddled over. "Holy shit! Are you okay?"

Shaking, I did my best to recount what had just happened. It felt like ages, but the whole thing had taken seconds. Psychic Midget offered to put me in the Shredder for the last quarter mile, but I declined. I wanted to get right back on the proverbial horse. I loved kayaking on the river, or at least everything that went with it: the sunshine, the elements, the camaraderie, camping with my friends. I pushed down the thought that I might be done, raised my right hand above my head and wiggled my fingers. "I think I can do this."

"What if you flip over again?"

"Aw hell, guys. If the river wants me that bad, I

guess it can have me."

. . .

A few days later, my shoulder dislocated when I tried to open my front door. Later that week, it popped out when I tried to pick up a book. Eventually it would come out if I wasn't careful enough getting out of bed. At Katie's urging, I saw a doctor, and then a specialist, and eventually a surgeon. The procedure was quick, but the recovery was most definitely not. After six months of physical therapy, I finally got back in the water.

But it just wasn't the same as before. That little tingle of glee I once felt at the top of a splashy part was replaced by softly jangling nerves. Worrying about making mistakes makes you make mistakes, and I made lots of them. But instead of overcoming them and improving my technique, all my focus now was on remaining calm and not losing my balance again.

In practice, even after the accident, I could "corkscrew" down the river. On long, flat stretches of water I would intentionally tip and roll, tip and roll, going under on one side, popping up on the other, drilling my way downstream like a rifling bullet until I grew tired or bored. But any time my balance shifted by surprise, I clutched at my skirt, ready to bail.

All progress had halted, and I was stuck as a "solid class II paddler, a little shaky on III." When I'm not moving forward, I get antsy. So while I kept all my gear, I only used it about twice a year. I still showed up for the hot tubs and bonfires, and sometimes I'd coast down a wide calm river just to be social. If the gang was going somewhere exciting, I would talk my way into riding shotgun in the Shredder, sipping sweet cider with Psychic Midget in the sun.

Until eventually we achieved the impossible and flipped the damn thing. And by we, I totally mean me. When you sit left rudder in the Shredder and the captain yells "turn," you should not have to ask, "Which way?"

It took years to dawn on me that maybe I never should have been on the water in the first place. Ah, but what a long fun process it was, finding out that I'm a land-based creature and should probably stick to walking.

■ ■ ■

Luckily for me, one of our favorite places to paddle was also a renowned hiking destination, the Nantahala Gorge in western North Carolina. The rafting outfitters are at the bottom of the gorge at the spot where the Appalachian Trail crosses the river. I'd seen the AT's signature white blazes painted on the bridge during numerous visits to paddle the nearby falls, and they reminded me of the ones I'd seen way back in my Marine days on a weekend trip to a trail near Quantico. That this was the same trail blew my mind. I felt its pull almost as strongly as the river's.

I asked about hiking on BoaterTalk and discovered lots of kayakers happy to throw on a pack after a day on the water. Our good friend Pimp offered to meet us at the gorge for a weekend hike on the AT. Pimp took us south toward Wesser Bald, and we spent a night at the A. Rufus Morgan Shelter, a three-walled structure made from logs and boards that resembled a cabin missing a wall.

The shelter was too small for the three of us to fit, so we decided to camp near a small stone fire ring downhill by a stream. I asked Pimp if all the shelters were so small, and he said he had no idea. Like most people who set foot on the Appalachian Trail, he usually spent only a day or two on it.

"It takes six months to do the whole thing," Pimp said. "Who has time for that?"

"I'd like to do it," I said.

"You should."

"Well, like you said, man. Who has time, right? Some day..."

The next day Pimp led Katie and me up to the fire tower on the top of Wesser Bald. He warned us that it was "a few steep miles," but those words did not adequately prepare us for the actual climb. The tower is on a peak more than half a vertical mile above the river—an impressive view, but a struggle to reach if you're accustomed to *sauntering* at sea level with a beer in your hand. Lugging 40 pounds of gear to the top (I hadn't yet heard of "ultralight") was brutal.

I sweat, I groaned, I stumbled, but I never complained. With every step our view improved, and with it my mood. From the tower we scanned a 360-degree view of an entire national forest.

Mist rose from the gorge and the wind cooled us. Sprawled on the platform with my arms and legs spread out, I closed my eyes and felt the tower sway in the breeze. It was almost like being in a hammock.

"I'm going to sleep up here tonight."

Pimp also thought that sounded fine, so he and I made camp right there. Katie descended and pitched her tent under some nearby trees, cautioning us that we were planning to sleep on top of a lightning rod.

I countered that the sky was completely blue and cloudless. "In fact, while you're down there," I called, "get me my sunscreen from my pack, would you?"

. . .

The first drops of rain hit my face around 5 a.m. It was only a light drizzle. I nudged Pimp, who was passed out and snoring beside me on the platform. "We should get down."

By the time we reached the bottom of the ladder, the rain was blowing sideways. By the time I got my tarp strung up below the tower, the lightning had started. And by the time we saw the sun again, hours later after we were halfway back down the mountain, it occurred to me that if I was going to do this instead of kayaking I would need a lot more practice.

CHAPTER 8
CLOUD CITY

IN 2007, THE SECOND anniversary card from Katie's mom arrived right on schedule. That year it had a note that asked, "Would you like to go on an adventure?"

Katie called her, and from the next room I could hear her side of the conversation. With each exclamation her excitement ratcheted up a notch.

"Would we? Heck yes!" ... "What, really?!" ... "This summer?" ... "YES! I'll tell Gary!"

I did my best to not interrupt until their call was over. "Tell me what?"

"Want to go to Peru?"

Ever since Katie's mom, Becky, learned about Machu Picchu in school, she has wanted to see it in person. Now that she was grown up and a schoolteacher herself, the middle of June seemed the perfect opportunity.

"Won't it be crazy hot?" I asked, picturing crumbling ruins in a steamy equatorial rain forest.

"Not at all. June is winter down there." And Machu Picchu was pretty far south, a thousand miles below the equator, and also high in the Andes Mountains.

"Aztec, right?"

"Inca."

Finally conceding that I didn't actually know much about the place, I let Katie give me the rundown. Machu Picchu was an old city, although not technically ancient. It was built by the Incas in the 1400s and abandoned not too long after, thanks to conquering Spaniards. For centuries its existence was rumored and the true location was known only to local farmers. An American named Hiram Bingham followed up on those rumors and brought it to international attention in 1912.

"As of now there are two ways to get there," Katie explained. "There's a teeny tiny town at the base of the mountain with a bus that goes up a windy road and takes you right to it. That's how Mom and Dad will go."

"Okay. And what's the other way?"

She grinned. "Four days on the Inca Trail."

■ ■ ■

I went into prep mode right away. We had six months to get ready, but there was still plenty to do. The first task was to get passports. My only "real" trip overseas had been a year in Okinawa back in the Marines, and I hadn't been out of the United States in over a decade. This was getting exciting! We brushed up on our Spanish, although everything we read said we wouldn't really need it. Shopkeepers, guides, and drivers all reportedly knew at least basic English, and most of our conversations would be spoken in numbers anyway. But I like to at least make an effort.

Katie surprised me with a few safety tips I wasn't expecting. One of the online reports she'd dug up suggested lining backpacks and purses with chicken wire. Apparently some of the more brazen pickpockets slashed at packs with knives, taking whatever fell out and running away. We agreed that this seemed unlikely—and that chicken wire lining was too much of a pain in the ass to bother with.

More reasonable warnings told of abundant stray dogs. "'If they do bother you,'" Katie read aloud, "'just throw stones. The strays have caught on, and now the mere motion of reaching for a rock usually sends them running.'"

"Good to know."

The days of following a farmer with a machete to the sacred city were long gone. An outfitter called Llama Path made regular excursions, had all the necessary permits, and provided porters to carry your gear for you. Guided hike or not, that notion made me nervous. The military had pounded into my head that my gear was my life. Being more than an arm's reach away from my kit meant a thrashing, so the idea of someone else carrying it for me was like picturing myself naked in the wilderness.

We worked out the timing so that we would be finishing our hike just as her parents arrived by train at Aguas Calientes, the small town at the bottom of the mountain. Then, with the logistics squared away, we now had to prepare for what would be our biggest challenge: the altitude.

Cusco, the former center of the Incan empire and the

city we'd be flying into, was at an altitude above 11,000 feet. Where we lived it was eight. Not eight thousand—eight feet above sea level. Making that jump would be hard on our bodies.

If you live at sea level, you start to notice the difference above 5,000 feet. I remembered that from our hike to the fire tower. The air a mile up is just a little thinner—not bad, but enough that you huff and puff a bit more than usual. Ten thousand feet is where you really feel it. You'll be winded constantly, perhaps even weak and nauseous. They say you can expect headaches and sleepiness. The lack of oxygen makes you feel hungover all the time. I'd been that far up once before, on a spring break ski trip to Colorado, but I had been drunk most of that week too, so the hangover feeling didn't really stand out in my memory.

Like a hangover, the best antidote for such a drastic and sudden change in altitude is time. A week or more was recommended. But we were still young and green enough at our jobs that we lacked the luxury of copious vacation time. We booked three days to acclimate at a hostel in Cusco, and that would have to do.

The next best alternative is cardiovascular fitness, so Katie drew up a training schedule for us. It involved lifting weights and running, with frequent visits to the stairs of a nearby parking garage, where we would simulate our upcoming challenge by hauling our backpacks to the top level repeatedly. After a few sessions we decided that we were wasting our time, and resorted instead to our previously established fitness routine of carrying plastic cups full of beer back and forth between Six Pence Pub and River Street.

A month away from leaving, Katie's mom called with disappointing news. She was having an issue with her blood pressure—nothing too serious, but the doctor had forbidden her from flying. Becky was grounded, which meant it was just going to be the two of us.

· · ·

We took the cheapest flight from Atlanta to Lima, Peru, where after clearing customs we switched to a much smaller prop plane with room for about a dozen passengers. In addition to skipping and shuddering over every little pocket of air, this plane did something unique in my experience: It went up, but didn't come down.

On every flight I'd ever taken, I had known we were near our destination when the plane began descending. For this flight we climbed out of Lima, reached cruising altitude, and stayed there, because that's how high Cusco is. They didn't even bother pressurizing the cabin; our ears popped as we ascended. The pilot wove skillfully among snowcapped Andean peaks. Several of us stared out our windows tensely as the plane veered directly toward one of the mountains.

We banked harder and circled around it, revealing a gray concrete ribbon with a few buildings at one end. It didn't feel like a landing as much as the earth rising up to meet us. Moments later I was on the tarmac, pulling my pack from a pile and panting.

"Why do I feel…like I just ran a marathon?" I gasped

to Katie.

It was worse than I'd expected. Walking the hundred yards or so to the taxi stand wore us out. We'd left home eighteen hours ago, and despite eating well on the jet plane, I was hungry. My mouth was dry and I was seeing spots.

"Do you feel as bad as I do?" I asked.

"I'm definitely foggy," she said.

On top of everything else, I was disoriented. It started with the flight that never came down, and was exacerbated by the unfamiliar sights and sounds. Background chatter in your native tongue, even when indistinguishable, is at least recognizable as words. Here in the echo chamber of the airport, it was all bright vowels and hard consonants. Horns were honking and someone was playing the pan flute. I felt like I didn't belong, like everyone but me was in on a joke.

A few steps out the door and we were swarmed by drivers offering, "Taxi, señor!"

We picked the one closest to the exit. In English he asked, "Where to?"

Katie read from her printed notes. "Loki Hostel, por favor!"

■   ■   ■

I'd never stayed in a hostel before. The first few I read about were actually just bunkhouses: nothing more than a long room full of beds much like my boot camp squad bay, except minus the drill instructors and filled with dirty hippies.

I was okay with that, but luckily Loki was nothing of the sort. A group of Irish backpackers had pooled their cash and purchased a crumbling 400-year-old hacienda, converting it into a hostel. Their restoration work was impressive. Solid timber beams supported the centuries-old ceilings. The floors were scarred hardwood, deeply stained and highly polished. Three-foot-thick stone walls kept our private room at 60 degrees, no matter what was happening outside. The large, sunny courtyard sported multiple hammocks, a few grungy backpackers, and someone's llama.

I wanted to begin exploring immediately, but my body had other plans. "I need to lie down for a second. My head...ugh."

"That's not a good idea," said Katie. "You're supposed to acclimate with gentle exercise. We should go for a walk."

"I know," I groaned. "But I want to lie down. Just for a second."

She joined me on the bed next to our bags. A gentle breeze brought me almost enough air. My head buzzed. I thought I heard a rooster out there. I was asleep in seconds.

■ ■ ■

We awoke an hour or so later to the sound of firecrackers and roosters crowing. I stumbled across the courtyard to look for the concierge. One unique feature of hostel travel is the concept of "work for stay"—guests on a budget can sometimes get a bed in exchange for, say, working the front desk. The place was basically empty since all the excitement was downtown, so I found our concierge swinging in a hammock, a fellow grubby backpacker.

"What's going on out there?" I inquired.

"Corpus Christi," she said. When I shrugged, she explained that it is one of the biggest religious holidays in the country. Sometimes it took all week. And this year, she explained, the parade would coincide with Inti Raymi, the Incan festival of the sun.

"You know, the solstice," she told me in a way that said it should have been obvious. "The first day of summer? Or I guess down here it's winter, right?"

The solstice! Of course! I'd spent the past six months reading about the Incan Empire, learning about Machu Picchu and why they built the place: They worshiped the sun. They even constructed a Temple of the Sun, where the sacred stones line up and cast shadows Indiana Jones-style on one day each year: the solstice.

The day we were supposed to get there. At sunrise!

"It all makes sense now!" I said, and thanked her.

"Yeah, no problem, man."

I ran back to our room and collapsed onto the bed. Katie was dressed and waiting. I was exhausted from the short jog, so the best I could do was mumble, "Parade...solstice...sunrise..."

She gave me a minute to recover and eventually I told her what I'd just learned.

"Did you ready any of the emails I sent you?" She asked.

I caught my breath and offered weakly, "There were so

many..."

She gave me her hand and said, "Come on, get ready. Let's head down there. It sounds like things are just getting good!"

■ ■ ■

Our hostel was at the top of a small hill, crowded among white buildings with terracotta roofs. None of the streets were straight, and some were so narrow we could almost hold hands from opposite curbs. Without obvious signs, we had to memorize our way back by landmarks. To get back to Loki, we'd need to turn left at the statue with water fountain nipples.

Cusco is a beautiful city, even when they're not in full party mode, which they were. Plaza de Armas lies at the center, a large landscaped square bordered by shops, restaurants, and venerable churches. Katie excitedly pointed out examples of Spanish colonial architecture while I marveled at the crowd gathered for the parade.

There were drums, horns and elaborate, brightly colored costumes. And that was just the spectators. Blocks away we could see the approaching chaotic procession. Masked men and women danced as teams, shouldering ornate palanquins bearing life-size replicas of famous saints. The saints themselves were decorated elaborately too. One mannequin bore a rosary in one hand and an inflatable SpongeBob SquarePants in the other.

When the parade reached the square, half of the spectators joined in. Old men and young women alike surrounded the floats and musicians. Young men danced with babies on their shoulders while children blew into real and plastic horns. One saint was being carried by people in rainbow-colored ski masks, while another was raised high by a hundred hands reaching to touch it at once. I felt more than one unknown hand brush against my back pocket too, making me glad I'd stashed my cash in my sock.

Once we thought the craziness had passed we heard another wave approaching. I couldn't tell if it was another parade or the same one making a second pass around the block. We were getting our appetites back, so we used this pause as our chance to cross the street and locate the source of a tantalizing aroma of roasting meat.

Our noses led us to an area full of long communal tables where revelers sat shoulder to shoulder devouring plates of bread, corn, vegetables, and crispy golden hunks of delicious looking barbecue. The area was shrouded in haze from the carts surrounding it. Each had their own fire, and what looked like more than enough food for everyone. We picked one at random and grabbed plates.

"Hola," I said.

"Hello! Have some cuy please, señor!"

He loaded my plate and Katie's. Only after I paid him did I notice that the barbecue still had eyes and teeth. I turned around and looked at the tables full of people eating barbecue that still had complete heads. Many meals still had feet. Too big to be a rat, I thought, but too small to be a dog.

"Señor," I asked, "what is 'cuy,' por favor?"

He smiled. "It is guinea pig. Enjoy!"

Katie shot me a look that said "roll with it," so I thanked him and we found a seat at the long tables.

"How are we supposed to eat this?" I asked.

She was equally dumbfounded. "I don't know. I read that the guinea pig is a delicacy here, but this doesn't look very delicate."

There it was again, that feeling that everyone was in on the joke but me. I watched for a bit, and saw that people were just picking the things up and gnawing on them like a turkey leg. That was a long way to go for a joke, I decided, so I joined in.

I picked up my guinea pig and tried to pretend it was chicken. I twisted off the back leg with some difficulty and sniffed it. "Smells like chicken," I said cautiously. "Even looks a little like a drumstick. Except this one has toenails."

"Mine still has fur," Katie added.

I closed my eyes and bit. The texture and flavor seemed at first like tough smoked chicken, though as I kept chewing, it began to resemble a piece of beef jerky that had been stashed in a leather glove and then tossed into a fire for ten minutes. But the high altitude appetite was upon us, and we gobbled up our guinea pigs.

We spent the next two days exploring the city, visiting ruins and restaurants. After cuy, the most daring thing we attempted was llama steaks, which were quite good. On the third morning we finally awoke without headaches, thanks to a combination of our youthful metabolism and coca tea. This delightful elixir is brewed from the leaves of the coca plant, the same one used for cocaine.

Coca tea offers none of the strong effects found in the illegal drug. It tastes great and delivers a slight buzz comparable to strong coffee, along with a relaxing of the brain's blood vessels, which eases the headaches brought on by altitude sickness. Locals have been brewing the stuff for centuries, and it is not uncommon to see older men or women with blackened teeth from a lifetime of chewing on the leaves. Unfortunately, it has no impact on lung capacity, so we were still huffing and puffing everywhere we went, albeit with slightly clearer heads.

At the top of one small peak overlooking the city we visited a ruin called Sechyahuaman, one of the earliest examples of Incan stonework. Another was a place called Qoricancha, the site of an ancient sun temple that now supported a magnificent baroque convent built by the Spaniards, Santo Domingo. The dividing line between architectural styles was stark, a solid foundation of carefully laid blocks placed by the indigenous people, mounted by a marvelous monument to splendor and excess. The place itself tells the tale of conquest just by its appearance alone.

As expected, we saw plenty of stray dogs, and as promised, they left us alone. No one tried to slash my pack, but we were pestered by throngs of street vendors, mostly children. One girl convinced Katie to buy two crocheted finger puppets, one for each hand. An instant after she paid for them, another child ran up and offered to sell her more. Katie told her she already had two. "But señora," the kid replied, "you have ten fingers!"

That night we returned to the hostel and rearranged

our gear, storing our suitcases in a locker at the hostel after we shifted a few basics into our backpacks. We weren't planning to get much sleep that night. Not because Corpus Christi was still raging, and not because our room was directly beneath the hostel's Irish pub, but because a van from Llama Path was picking us up to start the Inca trail at 3 a.m.

CHAPTER 9
DAY OF THE CONDOR

WE WERE SO EXCITED to start the trail that we barely slept a wink. The front desk had coca tea ready for us when we came down. We shivered as we stood out front in the dark, waiting for our van. The ride was silent until we were out of Cusco. Then everyone woke up because the van was bouncing so much. What little I could see by the van's headlights reminded me of old forest service roads, minus the trees, or the hastily gouged byways plowed by combat engineers in the desert. Someone had dragged a big machine through here some time ago, and scraped a wide, drivable swath that went... somewhere. There were no signs. The driver explained that we still had hours to go.

As the light gradually increased, it revealed an astonishingly dry plain sprawled among the peaks. Houses—dwellings, really—were rare and the space between them wasn't apparently being used for anything. Scrubby brown fields covered the lowlands between soaring piles of snowcapped rock. Of course, lowlands is a relative term; we had descended to a modest 8,000 feet during our approach to the trail's start.

The road improved as our driver took us into a long narrow valley, where we followed alongside the Urubamba River, a perfectly blue and white ribbon of roaring foam and big round rocks. Katie and I marveled at the wave trains, while the other two couples chatted among themselves. We hadn't been introduced yet, so I was relieved to hear them speaking English, although in accents I couldn't quite place.

This road was paved, and finally there were signs. None of them meant anything to me until I saw one which read CAMINO INKA, which meant we were near. Soon we pulled into a dirt lot with four other vans and a small crowd of locals.

One of them peeled off and approached us. He was a small man, the top of his head barely reaching my chest. He had a round face with a toothy smile and wore a knit cap, which he removed as he extended a hand. "Hello! I am Flavio. I will be your guide."

We introduced ourselves. Steph and Craig were from South Africa. David and Laura were an Aussie and a Brit. When Katie and I introduced ourselves as Americans, the other couples chuckled among themselves.

"We figured as much," said David. "Your packs, mate. You're the only ones lugging 'em." He indicated his entire load: a single water bottle dangling in a crochet pouch. I started to explain our rationale, but he did it for me. "You Yanks're fuckin' nuts, yeah?" This drew more laughter.

Flavio gestured to the crowd over by the other vans, a dozen or so young men of roughly his build. "These are your porters. They will be carrying everything you need for the next few days. Wave to them! You will not see them again until camp, which they will set up for us. If you want to give them your packs, señor and señora, now is your chance."

We still couldn't bring ourselves to part with our gear and politely declined. Flavio handed out trekking poles, something I'd never tried before, and we started down the Inca Trail.

■ ■ ■

We crossed the roaring Urubamba on a narrow footbridge and passed through a small kiosk, where we presented our passports. Then our group silently followed the river for the first half mile or so, which was unexpectedly dusty. I was surprised to see a cactus growing by the trail, and Flavio explained, "This part of the trail is desert. We will see many ecosystems. Tomorrow will be rainforest, but only after we climb very high today, up and over Dead Woman's Pass."

We all grimaced at the name, especially the ladies. "Why is it called that?" asked Steph.

Flavio laughed. "Not to worry! No one has died at this pass. But you might feel like it. You will see when we are up there. The outline of rock is shaped like a woman on her back."

He continued to tell us about the area while we walked, but I was distracted by the mountains that walled in the valley, colossal brown pyramids with bright white points that stood out painfully against the clear blue sky. My lollygagging combined with the weight of my pack slowed me down enough that I fell well behind the group. When I thought I could see the first set of ruins, I picked up my pace and caught the tail end of Flavio's explanation.

We were at Ayapata, the first real example of Inca stonework we'd encountered outside of Cusco. The precision was remarkable. Seeing this level of geometry way out here, miles from anywhere, left me breathless, and not just from the altitude.

Ayapata, Flavio was saying, is all that remains of an old Inca village. It was below us and on the opposite side of the valley, maybe a quarter mile away, but easy to see. At the bottom were the robust remains of stone buildings, exact rectangles and careful curves all of stacked smooth stone. Half of the opposite slope had been carved along the contour lines into roughly two dozen perfectly level steps with each rise carpeted in grass.

The illusion was disorienting. They were far away and huge, but looked near and small. Surely I could bound up those steps in a few quick hops. I fished my binoculars from my pack and zoomed in to find that there were stairs for people after all. They were tiny and zigzagged up the walls that supported the flat fields. Each level was probably 15 feet above the last.

"Why is this even here at all?" someone asked.

Flavio laughed. "Why is any village or town where it is?" He made a sweeping gesture. "This is all we have, so we work with it. That slope gets sun, and as you see, they made it flat for crops without removing the mountain. The river is not too far, so the Incas could bring the water."

Inca stonework was not limited to their homes, or for shoring up terraces. They also used it to irrigate. Stone-lined trenches carried water from the river a mile away. They even had separate systems for farming and drinking water, including a natural purification system for the latter. Aerated water is less likely to contain bacteria, so the Inca would route their supply through a series of cascading drops and fountains made of the same stones they used for everything else.

"What about roads?" I asked.

"You will see one," Flavio said. "The Inca trail is a road. Come, let's get back on it!"

I stowed my binoculars, retrieved my poles from the rock they were leaning against, and again hurried to catch up.

■ ■ ■

We were on the last flat stretch for a while. Katie and I lumbered with our packs while the other couples strolled ahead. Flavio did his best to keep the herd together by telling us about the Inca trinity of the condor, the puma, and the snake.

"They represent not spirits, but the three levels of consciousness," he said. "At the lowest, the snake is like what you call the id. It does not feel or think. It just eats and does what it must. Lots of people think the snake is bad. It is not, it is just low.

"Sometimes you will see the next level standing on the back of the snake. The puma, instead of eating the snake, he is riding on it. Puma is the conscious. Your senses, your thinking. Puma is life.

"The condor is the spiritual part. Its talons grasp the puma but he is not riding. He is carrying them both, even the snake which rides on the earth. The sacred trio links the earth to the sky."

I liked this interesting analogy, and could picture some Incan sitting alone on a mountain, learning all of this from his own version of my Spirit of the Woods.

Flavio continued. "It is also the sequence of life. The snake is your youth when you crawl on the ground. The puma is when you walk and hunt and make babies. The condor carries you to heaven. This was how Incas would dispose of their dead. The bodies would be carried to special mountains where condors will do the rest."

It was gruesome, but it made sense. Land was precious around here. Look at the lengths they went to just to grow corn. Precious acreage could not be sacrificed for burial. Why not let giant meat-eaters with 10-foot wingspans transport your loved ones off to the next world? No wonder these things were at the tops of the totems.

We were slowly gaining elevation and gradually more greenery surrounded us. The large mountain we'd been approaching for the last hour was getting bigger and I had been hoping we'd go around it despite knowing better. The path we were on disappeared into a lush tunnel of vegetation straight ahead. At its opening, the trail turned into crumbling steps.

Flavio stopped. "This is the road I told you about. All the ruins we will see, including Machu Picchu, were connected by these roads made of stone. All the villages and towns used them. It was their highways. While we are walking, I want you to think about how much work it took to make this."

The stairs were irregular. The rise and run of each step varied greatly, as did their levelness. I'd lift my foot about ten inches, place it, and take two full strides. Then I'd lunge upward a foot and a half a couple times, walk three strides and then up another six inches. Who built stairs like this? It got old fast.

"Hey Flavio," I called ahead. "What happened to all the precise Inca stonework here? This stuff's a mess!" And it was a pain to walk on too. Nothing at all like the close-fitting joints and polished corners back at Ayapata.

"The Inca way is to disturb the earth as little as possible. Where the mountain only goes up a little, they make a small step. And remember," he added, "these are over 500 years old, and were meant to be walked on each day. The Inca did not have to be so careful here because they knew they will replace the stone every few years."

I stopped on one of the shorter rises to catch my breath, leaned on my trekking poles, and felt my cheeks tingle. I was seeing spots, and when I patted my forehead with a cloth it came back dry. Heat exhaustion, altitude, or both? By now were back up around 9,000 feet I reckoned. The thin air and lack of clouds amplified the sun, so despite being almost winter, it felt like summer. I drank and moved on.

Katie was up ahead almost out of sight, executing the same technique she had on all of our practice hikes—turtling. Head down, never stopping. Flavio fell in behind me, taking the sweep position and distracting me from my labored breathing with more stories about the Inca. Suddenly I detected the rumble of many approaching feet. "Chaskis!" he called out, waving at me to step aside. "Porters!"

A herd of young men stampeded by, the same ones from the vans earlier, now decked out in matching "Llama Path" T-shirts. The tallest, a six-footer, led the pack. Most wore sandals, a few were barefoot, and there wasn't a trekking pole in sight. Instead of packs, each bore a canvas sack slung over one shoulder, Santa Claus-style. They were monstrous, almost cartoonish in size, some bigger than the men carrying them, their contents bulging and clanking as the train hustled by.

There were only six tourists, and two of us were carrying our own gear. I puzzled over how our group needed 19 people. Flavio anticipated my question. Still smiling, he said, "Here is why everybody thinks of America as being all cowboys. I see so many people from around the world, so I know you have a different way to do things. It is good, really, to want to do everything yourself. Tonight you will learn a new way for camping. Let us do something for you. This is our way."

He clearly wasn't going to tell me what was in the bags, so we changed the subject. I needed to stop more frequently, and within an hour we had lost sight of the rest of the gang. Flavio ran ahead to check on them, and in the 15 minutes he was gone, I tried Katie's turtle style and managed to only need six breaks.

"How far ahead are they?" I asked when he returned.

"Oh, about a mile." He was barely panting.

"That means you just *ran* two miles? Up here?" I was dumbfounded. "How?"

"I would offer to carry your pack, but I know your answer, señor." He gestured and I continued climbing the stairs.

My lungs were becoming useless. Each deep breath felt weak and unfulfilling, like I had clogged nostrils or the flu. My quads cramped and my calves quivered, even my arms were starting to tire from pulling myself up each crazy step. And it was steps all the way to Dead Woman's Pass.

I looked up from turtling and saw more stairs. Then I looked back past Flavio and got so dizzy I had to sit. The view literally knocked me off my feet. We had climbed nearly half a mile in altitude, the same as the fire tower back home, but instead of zigzagging up through a green tunnel, we'd stomped our way up the spine of a sky-high pyramid.

We'd left the treeline behind a while ago, but I'd been zoned out, staring at my shoes. Now I could see one of the chocolate-colored mountains we'd previously stared up at with amazement was now well below us. There was another behind it, and behind that another still. Some snow and ice covered the very top, making the whole thing appear to be a giant fudge sundae. I needed to eat.

While I searched my pack for a granola bar, Flavio

pointed halfway down the mountain into a deep dark groove. "This is where the glacier used to go," he said.

"When?" I asked. "Like a million years ago? Or when the Inca were here?"

"It was always here. My grandfather and his grandfather remembered it. It began melting when I was a boy." He paused. "We should go. There is still far for us to climb."

. . .

It was practically paved the whole way. I considered what went into building this trail, this road, this never-ending staircase. The idea of lugging rocks around up here and chiseling them into right angles for stacking made my chest burn just thinking about it.

"Flavio," I asked, "do you guys grow a third lung or something from being up here all the time?"

"This is like normal for us," he said. "Did you see how the porters ran by us? Zoom! Llama Path has a race every year to see who can do the whole Inca Trail the fastest. Guess how fast is the record."

Our trail route was just under 30 miles. We were taking a few days, but I didn't imagine someone in a race would have that luxury.

"A day?" I guessed.

"Eight hours."

"What?! You've got to be kidding me."

"Not me, of course. I need a whole day. But one of these guys," he motioned ahead, "they can bring some water and a snack and run from the Urubamba to Aguas

Calientes from breakfast to dinner."

I whistled, which made me dizzy. "Now I don't feel so bad about them hauling…whatever's waiting for us at the top of the mountain."

Flavio smiled. "Now you see!"

■   ■   ■

More up. I had stopped being impressed long ago and now felt next to nothing. I was sweating again, which was good, but now we were high enough for cold winds. For a second I thought the Spirit of the Woods was whispering to me, but when I looked up there were no trees. In a hypnotic daze, I imagined being watched by the unblinking eye of an indifferent sun god. Maybe I'll see a condor soon, I thought. He can carry me to the top, or just carry me off. Either way I'm good.

Late in the afternoon, the mountain intervened between us and the sun. The instant it was obscured I missed it. The temperature dipped a cool ten degrees and I yearned for heat despite my sweat. I could only imagine what night would bring.

My head was buzzing now, my eyes practically shaking in their sockets. I felt hungover and weak, and instead of walking I was bumbling and shuffling. My hands were blistered from leaning on my poles. But all of this was happening somewhere in the distance, not to me but to my body. Pain signals were being noted, filed, and disregarded by my oxygen-starved brain. Nothing hurt and I was floating up the mountain, grinning like an idiot.

I heard laughter ahead. That's the dead woman, I thought. It was.

The backlit silhouette in the direction of the setting sun was indeed that of a giantess in repose. I could see her forehead, nose, and chin, pointing upward as if gazing at the now emerging stars. The small round cliff of her chin dropped off sharply into a long flat neck of exposed rock, slender and smooth.

Flavio pointed. "There is her breast. That rock is the nipple. Come—camp!"

The day's final horizon hugged us in close like the walls of a small stadium. The laughter was coming from tents lined up along the low sheltered base of the ridge opposite us, and Flavio bounded off toward them and was greeted with hugs by a few of the porters. There were so many tents it was like a military base camp—but multicolored, no one was yelling, and something smelled delicious. In other words, nothing like a military base camp.

I found Katie in our group's circle of tents and called out to her as I limped over. "Do I smell popcorn?"

"You do!" she said. "Get in here. Are you okay? We were worried about you until Flavio started running reports for us. Here, have some coca tea."

I took off my boots and switched to sandals. "Where'd all these people come from?" I asked and sipped the tea. Almost instantly my temples stopped throbbing.

"This is all our stuff," she said. "We're the only ones up here, our group and the porters. You should see what they did. There's a dining tent, like with tables and chairs. They brought an entire *kitchen,* Gary!"

"I have to see this."

"Follow the smell of popcorn."

Craig and Steph, along with Laura and David, were seated around a table for six set with china, metal utensils, and a small candle burning beside a large bowl of steaming popcorn. David indicated the two empty chairs. "Drop yer ass on that, mate. Fuckin' delightful!"

The six of us ate handfuls of popcorn while the porters—now wearing white chef jackets—brought us more tea and bowls of soup.

"This is insane," I said. "Did you guys know it was going to be like this?"

"We did," Craig said. He and Steph said they'd been on similar trips in South Africa. "This is one of the best though, for sure."

"How long you on holiday for, yeah?" Laura asked Steph.

Craig and Steph looked at each other and shrugged. "I think this is week three or four, right?" said Steph. "Not sure what day it is, really. We're off to Brazil next. We're doing six total though. And you?"

David put his arm around Laura and beamed. "We're doing six too mate, only not weeks. Six months, yeah! Square in the middle of it too. No idea what's next!" He hugged her tighter and she smiled.

"Nice!" Craig said, then looked at me. "What about you then, eh?"

I stammered so Katie picked it up. "Oh, we're just taking two weeks. Well, ten days really. So after this, I guess it's back to work."

I saw what I interpreted as real pity. There was no meanness behind it, but we were clearly out of our league here. People our age who took entire months off, or *half a year* off, had to be millionaires, CEOs, or trust fund babies.

"Speaking of which," I said, hoping to lighten things up a bit, "what do you guys do?"

Neither couple wanted to go first, and when David finally broke the silence his answer surprised me. "Well right now, fuckin' nothing, right, babe?" Laura laughed and nodded.

"Yeah, you Yanks—sorry mate, Americans," he continued. "You always lead with that question too, like work's so important you model everything around it. Everything from conversations to your whole lives, right? I wash dishes, mate. I scrub fuckin' pots and pans when I can, and I love it. Me and my sheila here, we get a shit flat for a few months out of the year, work our asses off, and spend the other half doing shit like this."

"Us too," Steph said. "We do shorter holidays, but more each year."

"So where's home?" I asked. "And how long do you do this for? When are you done and what's next?" I had more questions. I was intrigued.

"Easy, mate." David said and raised his water glass. "We stop wherever we are when we run out of money." He winked.

"We're in Greece for a bit," Craig said. "Not sure about next year."

Amazed, I turned to Katie. "Why don't we do something like this? Surely there's some way…" I trailed off. Our living room wasn't quite kayaks and milk crates anymore. We had a lease and a couch. I had a desk. "Maybe in a few years."

Katie agreed that that sounded fun, and soon the subject changed to other things: what we saw that day, and how hard the climb was. The views! And the stairs! I wasn't even sore or tired anymore. Maybe it was the tea, but my head felt clear again. Nevertheless I was distracted for the remainder of our conversation. The idea of finding a job that would let me travel more kept surfacing. I tried to be in the present and enjoy the meal and the company, but I was silently scheming.

Now there was freshly squeezed lemonade, brought to us in tinkling glasses. Somehow, there was ice. It looked like it had been chipped from a block, and while I was savoring the sweetness, our main course arrived — a plateful of llama filets and steaming vegetables and rice. We dined there at the table in our candlelit tent above 13,000 feet, while outside the sky blazed with unfamiliar stars.

Eventually the endorphins wore off and I could feel my legs again. Everyone was yawning and the candle was a stub. Flavio blew it out and wished us a good night as we shuffled off to our tents. I dreamed of a large bird with soft black wings who scooped me up gently and carried me away to far off lands.

CHAPTER 10
TEMPLE OF THE SUN

THE NIGHT BROUGHT ICE. As the porters outside laughed and chattered, I watched my breath rise to the roof of our tent, where it had condensed into a layer of tiny crystals. Soon there was a crunch of approaching footsteps, and Flavio tapped gently on our tent, shaking loose some of the frost into flurries that settled and melted on my cheeks. "Good morning," he said. "Who wants coca tea?"

"Two, gracias," Katie mumbled, and unzipped the tent flap just enough for him to hand us each a steaming tin mug. It was delicious. My ears stopped ringing and I could breathe. When I stood up, I didn't even see spots. Maybe we were finally getting used to the air.

By the time we made it to the dining tent, the eggs and pancakes were almost ready. The porters offered us fresh popcorn with butter while we waited.

"Where's Craig?" I asked Steph. "Still in his bag?"

"He left before sunrise with one of the porters," she said. "He's going to try and make it all the way today."

I was impressed. The plan called for two more full

days plus a wakeup, though at least most of it was downhill. "Wow," I said. "Sounds pretty ambitious."

"Yeah, well," she said, her look turning serious. "He's hoping to find a doctor."

"Oh no! What for?" I asked.

"He was up all night, uh…" She made quotes with her fingers. "Using the bathroom."

David peered over his mug at us and sipped. "Sounded like it was coming out of both ends."

Katie and I had been out cold and thankfully hadn't heard any of the disturbance. But we were pretty sure of the cause: contaminated water. Craig had been refilling his bottle straight from the springs and streams, which were not the same as Inca fountains. Drinking it unfiltered was a bad idea. Now he needed antibiotics.

Backtracking was out of the question; there was nothing down there but the river and a checkpoint. A small camp town lay a few miles ahead, but it had no medical services either, just a few locals selling food and scarves. Craig's best bet was to make it all the way to Machu Picchu before sunset and catch one of the tour buses back down to Aguas Calientes, which equaled more than a 20-mile day. Doable in good health, but not something I'd want to attempt facing dehydration.

"Must not be too worried if you didn't go with him," I said, and Steph confirmed. We changed the subject and devoured breakfast before packing up and stepping off.

The porters stayed back to break camp while we climbed the rest of the way up and over Dead Woman's Pass. From the top we could see their red shirts dotting the scrubby flats below, scurrying about folding and stowing, filling those ridiculous sacks. It won't be long until they zoom right past us, I thought.

Up here, a few hundred feet above the camp, it was mostly rocks. At nearly 14,000 feet we'd left the tree line long ago. Now we were at the vegetation line. Among the occasional tufts of rugged tall grass or tough lichen I'd occasionally spot a purple flower or two. Otherwise it was brown and bouldery. Another thousand feet up would be snow, but we were done going up. The pass took us over the ridge and down the opposite side.

Before we descended I looked back one last time. I would not see that view again. But new peaks lay ahead.

In fact, it was all peaks. Not the round grassy humps we called mountains back home. These were pointy and loomed. All the way to the horizon we were at eye level with skyscrapers of rock, jagged like glass, white with snow.

The day warmed quickly and the steam from the valleys rose to meet us. It was still a bit misty when we reached our next stop, the Inca ruins called Pacaymayu. Though that word misrepresents their present condition; these structures were nearly livable. Yesterday I'd scanned Ayapata through my binoculars, but here I could actually touch the stone. There were no plaques or rope barriers, just us and a mossy maze.

We set down our packs and poles and wandered, gaping, astonished. The 500-year-old walls stood straight and strong at precise right angles. Many had deep rectangular peepholes that at first seemed cut through them, but that upon closer examination were precise gaps in the carefully stacked stone, exact openings that had been designed and worked around.

More amazing was that the Inca who built Pacaymayu didn't use bricks. These walls looked—and worked—like a jigsaw puzzle. No two blocks were the same, and they interlocked at crazily canted angles, making no sense at all until you came to an edge, where the pieces dovetailed smoothly into orderly walls, doors, and stairs. Every crazy joint fit flush. The Inca used no mortar, relying on the shape and weight to hold everything in place. Half a millennium later, you still couldn't slip a sheet of paper between the blocks.

Only the roofs were missing, which made it seem like exploring a petrified hedge maze. Flavio explained that the original roofs were similar to thatch, high pitched to shed any snow. Heavy rain wasn't really a problem up here. The peaks were full of rough grass that grew faster than they needed it. We'd get to see at Machu Picchu, where a small section had been restored for study and display.

We continued hiking down through the mist and into one of the deep flowery places between the peaks. The trail was still mostly uneven stone stairs, but their consistency was improving. In a few places the Inca had constructed tunnels where it was impossible to go over or around.

"Think about driving to any modern city," Flavio said. "The roads get better and wider as you get close to it. The buildings too. Ayapata that you saw yesterday? That is what you would call 'way out in the country' for the Inca. Here we are kind of in the suburbs. Machu Picchu was a very busy part of the Inca empire for a long time. It was the big city. You will see how different it is."

After a few more hours of downhill the slope leveled out again. We were far enough under the mist now that it seemed just a cloudy day. Stairs gave way to a paved path carved into the side of a high slope. I could see another site ahead, perched on a cliff. We were at Sayaqmarka.

"Curious things here," Flavio said. "Come, look!"

First we saw a fountain, which was more like a sink: a long, smooth groove carved into a flat rock countertop so polished and straight it looked as if a team of contractors had hauled in generators and compressors and diamond-tipped drill bits with laser levels. Nope. A handful of dudes from the jungle took turns chipping at it for most of the summer 500 years ago. Their buddies did the same a few feet uphill. They snaked their way to the top, extending the grooves and vertical drops to a natural spring or permanent snow melt high above. Their plumbing was open for easy access, always clean, and made of rock which over centuries had yet to significantly erode.

Flavio also pointed out handholds smoothly carved into the wall beside the steps, which might mean Sayaqmarka was a place for the Inca elderly. That they built safety walls along the edges here, and nowhere else, told that there might have been plenty of toddlers too.

Once again we heard the familiar rumble of passing porters. They were still on the paved part of the trail and weren't stopping to marvel at fountains or handholds. There was popcorn to be popped. As their cloud settled I paused to wonder how they got those packs through the tunnels back up there in the mist.

Camp was set up when we arrived, and again dinner was impressive. By dark our porters were a full dozen again. Craig's runner returned just as we were bedding down. He had put Craig on a bus and then run back 10 miles to let Steph know, finishing a 30-mile day with a smile. The news made her smile too.

■ ■ ■

After another day of going up and over ridges, wandering through ruins, losing altitude, and eating popcorn, we were nearing Machu Picchu and could tell. The quality of stonework in the trail and the ruins increased, as did their size. Winay Huayna, our penultimate stop, looked like a medieval castle on the stage of an amphitheater, with dozens of farming terraces of uniform height. Buildings had more rooms, and some were two stories, with cutouts where wood beams had once supported ceilings and attics. Gone were the jigsaw pieces; here the oddly shaped blocks were stacked in level rows. Far below rushed the Urubamba, another clue that we were close. Machu Picchu was just over the next ridge.

That night we had our final camp with Flavio and the porters. Before we entered the dining tent, he held an informal ceremony to acknowledge the crew and show our gratitude. Each of us took a turn voicing our admiration, and during dinner we privately signed a group card and stuffed it with cash, as is the custom.

Flavio would pass it to the head porter to distribute later.

"The porters will not sleep tonight," he told us. "Breakfast is at 3 a.m. We must start early to reach the Sun Gate by dawn. When we get down, it will still be an hour of daylight before the sun clears the mountain. There are many places to see something special when that happens. And because it is the solstice, Inti Raymi, there will be celebrations."

We were arriving on June 21, the shortest day of the year in the southern hemisphere. Of course it would have meant something to the Inca, who worshiped the sun and lived by their crops. The return of life-giving light is a significant moment for every developing culture, and learning to time it accurately was an achievement. Celebrating it with monuments was the next level.

It had been dark for a while. Sunlight was indeed scarce, and it got cold fast. Katie and I put on hats and mittens. It wasn't exactly freezing, but we were still accustomed to Savannah nights.

■ ■ ■

We were also accustomed to a slightly later wakeup call, but again, a warm tin of coca tea eased our woes.

The waxing moon had set hours ago, and with the sun still hours off, our final walk to the dining tent was cold, dark, and dewy. When we pulled aside the flap, a burning candle revealed that our porters had baked us a three-layer carrot cake with butter cream frosting and decorative piping like Machu Picchu at sunrise. All nineteen of us got a slice.

As we climbed the final ridge, my world was reduced to the cone of light emitting from my forehead. I could hear the gang ahead of me, rustling through branches, warning of roots. Bugs crowding my headlamp cast large shadows on Katie's pack as she turtled through the tunnel of brush.

We climbed smooth stairs through wild vegetation. We were now at 7,000 feet, below the altitude of Cusco. That explained the humidity. Everything dripped. I looked up to check if the sky had cleared, but only saw a dimly lit circle of leaves. I swatted a moth. We walked.

When we stopped, I thought we were lost. The trail unexpectedly opened into a wide paved area peppered with kiosks. Through the gloom I saw a series of walled terraces and a tall stone gate.

"Inti Punku!" Flavio exclaimed. "The Sun Gate!"

My disoriented feeling came from the sheer size of the place. I thought at first we'd wandered into a modern structure built for tourists, but no—this was centuries old yet still looked new. The gate was a simple rectangular opening at the top of a long, wide stairway—more of a dais really.

I stood between the blocks with Katie and the others. The sky was already brightening in the east, and the mountains in the west caught the glow with their snowy tops, casting it back as pink, then peach, then white. Below, the valley unveiled itself from the shadows, oozing from black to foggy emerald. The sky above was silvery and overcast. We might not get the sun. I shivered.

Flavio pointed us toward the center of a vast bowl formed by ridges, each one a jagged curved saw blade made of earth. Mist circled their tops. I squinted to see, in the middle of it all, Machu Picchu.

The city sprawls atop a pointed cone of boulders and grass, like the collector at the center of a radar dish miles wide. Even in the predawn light it was easy to spot. Its right angles and perfect curves stood out against the rippling lush chaos, each building a jewel set in a magnificent crown.

The sense of remoteness was profound. I knew that the modern town of Aguas Calientes sat at the base of the mountain on the other side—I could see the winding road—but up here everything was green and steaming. From horizon to horizon was nothing but bushy peaks. No signs of civilization for miles in any direction but for the engineered marvel of rocks and rectangles at the bottom of the slope before us. It was obvious why this was numbered among the Seven Wonders of the World.

Flavio snapped us out of our trances. "Come, we must hurry. To the Temple of the Sun!"

We still had about half a mile to go before entering the city, and as the trail approached it, the true magnitude of the site became a reality. The perspective of distance had made the location seem cozy, bordering on cramped, even through my binoculars. From within, the city was too big to see from any one spot.

We had some time to explore as the wind sluggishly pushed the mist around. It was still a little overcast but the light was increasing. Flavio showed us what the Inca used as their quarry. In one corner of the city is a pile of boulders, about three acres of granite. That served as an excellent source for building materials not just because of its endless tonnage, but because it was just uphill of the living area. When it was time to begin work on another part of the city, enormous blocks of stone could be broken off and rolled to their desired location.

Beside a chunk the size of a car, Flavio showed us which rocks were used for tools and which were blocks, solely based on their hardness. Workstations had been made from huge slabs that protruded from the earth, never moved by man. Flavio called this "using the nature rock," and repeated that phrase several more times, mostly about monuments. If the Inca found a beautiful or useful boulder, he explained, they believed it was there for a reason and would not move it. That would be the site of a stage or an altar, or in one case, the likeness of a soaring condor made from the nature rock itself.

In the city center, now filling up with people coming in from the Aguas Calientes side, Flavio said we would see three things: the Temple of the Sun, the Room of Three Windows, and Inti Watana, "Hitching Post of the Sun." These architectural marvels were each designed to line up and cast shadows in a certain way on this day only. A short walk separated the three, and space was filling up as the sky brightened and the tourists from the valley spilled out of the buses and into the temples.

Steph broke away in a dash. She had spotted Craig on one of the terraces below and was calling to him as she ran. Their gleeful reunion reminded Katie and me of her parents, who might have been here too. We'd have to bring them something special. Someone licked my elbow.

Startled, I spun, coming face to face with a friendly llama. He made a move for my chin, and when I flinched he chose some tall grass instead.

"These are who keep the place mowed," Flavio laughed, releasing us to explore on our own. The sun would crest over the towering spike of a ridge at any moment, so if we wanted a good spot we should hurry.

The Temple of the Sun looked like the turret of a medieval castle. Spiraling stonework here resembled masonry I was more familiar with, featuring level rows and alternating bricks. There were more trapezoids and the blocks were bigger and smoother, the fits somehow tighter.

People were shoulder to shoulder at the temple and there was no way in. We opted to remain in the open next to the Room of Three Windows—actually just a wall. But another polished, expertly built one, smooth to the touch, probably by design but also from centuries of caressing to see if it really was that smooth. In the wall, as you would guess by its name, were three large windows. Thirty or so feet directly west of the center opening stood a monolith.

A man and woman in elaborate headdress, adorned with beads and carrying drums, stepped through the crowd, which gave them a wide berth. Flavio's hand appeared and tapped my shoulder. "Old priest and priestess," he whispered. "They will read the ceremony in Quechua, the old language."

They began chanting, slowly at first. Beyond the

windowed wall, a steep drop into nothing. A mile of empty air above it lay between us and a towering spike of leafy steaming rock, backlit by the climbing sun. Beams of light shone from behind that summit, creating a golden aura that radiated from all sides. We were directly in the center of the mountain's shadow as it eclipsed the sun, which had baked off most of the mist. The sky behind it was now blue with yellow streaks of light.

I could still see my breath and my cheeks were rosy. All day since waking in the dark I had been craving the sun's warmth, and here in a sacred spot devoted to its very worship, the arrival was going to be delayed as long as possible. It seemed like a cruel tease. Checking behind me, I could see those peaks were lit—glowing, in fact. It was nice and warm up there.

I urged the sun to hurry up, bouncing and whispering, "Come on, please," as if the sun somehow had the capacity to listen or the will to comply. I was even prepared to thank that blazing ball of hydrogen if it ever appeared. *This is how worship starts.*

And then it hit me. The towering peak held onto the dark until the last possible second, and when that white fire exploded at the very top, my eyes couldn't take the brilliance. My gaze was forced down, directed at my feet, instantly humbling me. I was not built to see this. No one was. Instead I saw the shadow of the peak, a dark carpet stretched out before me, slowly pulling away as the light climbed higher.

This only happens here, I thought. Right here. When the top corner of the mountain's shadow receded all the way to the cliff, the Wall of Three Windows exploded into shining fire. The lone monolith was bathed in light. In another part of the city, a beam crossed the hard eye of a stone condor. The priests chanted faster and shook their beads, while a young man with dreadlocks danced beside me, crying and smiling and waving his hands at the sun. He was wearing earbuds, and when I leaned in close I was not surprised to detect some Pink Floyd.

Katie smiled and squeezed my hand. Behind her I could see the shadows of every building—there are over 200 of them—all lined up exactly with the walls of their neighbors or with their crop terraces. Every single one of them. The llamas wandered and chewed, unaware that they were standing in a giant observatory.

Before the Inca ever arrived, before anyone chipped a single flake, the sun hit this spot, in this magical way, and only on this day. What a location for a civilization that lived for the light. The whole mountain was as much a temple as that lovely structure below us on the hill, where everyone was applauding the sun.

■   ■   ■

Over the next several hours we climbed terraces and beheld spectacles and flowing fountains, more llamas and more sunshine. Soon, too much sunshine, really. I was getting burned. More crowds were arriving from Aguas Calientes, and we'd seen enough. The hike and the altitude, the early rise and the cold had all taken their toll. It was barely noon and we were yawning. I took a nap in some shade. Katie slouched beneath a tree. Some tourists did yoga nearby. You'd never guess that the solar system had just aligned only hours ago.

We lost our group in the crowd, but that was okay. We were finished, and goodbyes weren't really necessary. We ran into Flavio again that evening down in Aguas Calientes. We shared a pizza and wished him well. The next morning we took the train back to Cusco.

The ride back took a few hours, and I used that time to think about what I'd seen. My expectations had been blown away on this trip. Though long gone, the Inca spoke to me in a way. They found their spirit and their balance in the mountains, and I could relate.

Exploring. Exploring was the answer. It usually was for me. Even though we'd just spent a week in a far off land, climbing to new heights, touching ruins, somehow I wanted more. To be somewhere on our own. To see not just things that were rare, but actual *new things*. Places where no foot had ever stepped, no shutter had ever snapped.

Such places don't exist, I thought. At least not on any maps that I have.

It felt strange to be moving so fast. The mountains rushed by in reverse, behind plowed fields and the distant misty river.

CHAPTER 11
HOME IS FORWARD

"Marco!"

From somewhere up ahead I barely heard my wife reply, "Polo!" This was a surprise, not because we were playing the classic swimming pool game on a rocky, overgrown gorge in Newfoundland, but because I thought she was behind me.

Katie waited while I climbed through thick vegetation, inching toward the sound of her voice. I didn't bother asking how our marching order got shuffled. On any normal trail we would have noticed the leapfrogging, but not here. Where we were, there were no trails.

When I got close enough to spot her, we stopped, sweating freely under our head nets, which kept out ceaseless, blinding swarms of black flies. I balanced on a muddy rock and leaned into the branches of thick, stunted pines which caught in my pack straps. Katie leaned on her poles and peered into the distance, and said she could almost see Mark.

A faint holler came from ahead, though I couldn't

pick it out over the rustle of my head net and the buzzing in my ears. "What did he just say?"

"I couldn't hear, but I think he's breaking out the GPS," she replied.

Again? I thought.

Mark, the brains behind this ridiculous excursion, is a much faster hiker than Katie or me, despite his slightly shorter stride and the extra 25 pounds of camera equipment he usually carries. I have the longest stride, but was now bringing up the rear thanks to frequent stops to take pictures with my less bulky pocket camera. After about the tenth time I'd used my outside voice to shout, "Hold on! I'm too far back to hear you!" Katie came up with the idea of using "Marco Polo" as a fun way to put the brakes on whomever was in the lead. It had fewer syllables, and it served to remind us that this was supposed to be fun.

I ran the bite valve of my Camelbak under my bug net and sipped water while we waited. The rumble of the waterfall, our goal, was definitely in front of us somewhere. Its muffled roar had been our direction of travel for nearly an hour, and we had occasionally caught glimpses of it.

But thick brush now prevented any clear line of sight greater than five feet, so it was impossible to tell how far it was—and more importantly, whether we were approaching it from the correct side.

While ascending on the right side would be extremely difficult, we knew doing so on the left was impossible. If we made the wrong approach, a long backtrack and course correction would await us, with more miles and more flies.

■ ■ ■

On New Year's Day in 2010, my wife approached me with an odd request. "Do you remember Mark?" she asked.

Sure, I remembered Mark. "You mean Laughing Totem, right?" We had bumped into him several times over the years at various kayaker gatherings. We had one of his landscape photos framed on our living room wall. And now that I thought about it... "Don't we still owe him money?"

"I think you're right. Anyway, he made this post last night, and it caught my eye: 'Just throwing this out there. Anyone want to come play in the tundra this summer?' There's a link to something called the Long Range Traverse."

She passed me her laptop and what I first saw on her screen didn't look real—more like an oil painting of the Cliffs of Insanity from *The Princess Bride*. Row after row of massive cliffs and fjords interlocked like the teeth of colossal gears, as rough seas lapped angrily at their lower slopes. One of the towers was cracked, and from the cleft spewed a sky-high waterfall which never reached the bottom, but dissolved into a rainbow-filled mist halfway down.

"What planet is this?" I asked.

"Newfoundland," Katie said. "And that's just the view from the start of the hike! Hard to get to, though. It's the Long Range Mountains in Gros Morne National

Park, on the western end of the island. There's a ferry tour of the fjords, and you buy a special one-way ticket where they kick you off the boat at the turnaround point. Then you have to climb a waterfall."

She took her computer back and clicked a few things. "The only trip report I could find so far says to stay to the right of the falls."

"Trip report? Are you already researching this?"

I had to admit, it looked fun. Maybe even a little dangerous. I looked over her shoulder. "It says right here there aren't any trails." That made me want to go even more. "How much do you trust me with a map and compass? Should we consider this?"

"I already told him yes."

This made me glad. It had been a few years since the Inca Trail, our last big trip together. I was itching to put my pack on again, to visit a strange new place and eat weird stuff, maybe even get lost.

"When is this happening? And what do we really know about this Mark guy? We've only really met him like, what, two or three times? How do we know he's not a creep? That's a long time to spend with someone you barely know. And how long is this Long Range Traverse?"

"Depending on what route we take, 30 to 40 miles."

Forty miles might as well be a million. I was years away from seriously considering the Appalachian Trail, and 40 miles then seemed like an insanely long distance to carry a backpack. As it should seem to any reasonable person.

"Anyway, you're right," Katie continued. "We

should at least make sure we don't hate each other. That's why we're going to have lunch with Mark and Sue this weekend."

• • •

They drove two hours to meet Katie and me at a pub in Asheville. While we sipped our beers, it became obvious that Mark wasn't some weirdo planning to lure us into the wilderness and chop us into little pieces. Occasionally in life, you meet someone you hit it off with right away. Within the first 10 minutes of our lunch date, Mark had already referenced Douglas Adams, J.R.R. Tolkien, and six awesome bands from the '80s, including two I somehow hadn't heard of. When we'd met before on the river, Mark used cool terminology that kind of intimidated me, words like "gnarly" and "bomber." Here he was saying things I could totally relate to, words like "Frodo" and "dungeonmaster." We hadn't even ordered yet and we were already interrupting and finishing each other's sentences. Katie and Sue rolled their eyes in unison.

Mark worked as a graphic designer, and Sue was a professor of biology at a nearby university. She was outdoorsy, no doubt, but lacked that trait which makes some of us want to spend days or weeks there, and would not be accompanying us on the Long Range Traverse. But she shared our enthusiasm to know more, including also secretly wanting to verify that Katie and I weren't luring Mark to *his* grisly demise. She looked across the table and asked, "You guys know what you're getting into?"

"Just the basics," Katie answered. "Why don't you fill us in on the specifics?"

Mark swallowed two large gulps of beer and leaned in. "Alright. I figure we should shoot for the beginning of September. The black flies should be mostly gone by then. They don't take a chunk out of you like horseflies, but they bite—they're like gnats on steroids."

"They have 'em up in Maine. They swarm like mosquitoes," Katie said.

"Right," Mark continued. "They number in the millions. They'll slow you down for sure. Do you guys have head nets? You should get some. Bug spray is useless, plus we'll sweat it off. Anyway, we should go in September because the flies will be gone, and it should still be kind of warm. The Long Range Traverse is tundra, and they only allow permits during thaw, which isn't long."

"Permits?"

Katie frowned at me. "Did you read any of the links I sent you?"

I blushed. "What's that going to cost us?"

"Not much," said Mark. "There's a fee, but the hard part is our group has to pass a written navigation test. Gary, this is where you come in. Katie says you're good at that?"

I blushed again. Land navigation was definitely my strong suit. I am an actual bona fide expert, having taught that very subject to battalions of Marines during my decade of service. I was so adept at finding hidden metal boxes in the hundreds of square miles of swamp surrounding Quantico that they eventually let me be the guy holding the clipboard while other people scoured through the brambles.

"I'll give it my best shot," I said.

"Cool. I know how to navigate, I just suck at test taking. Once we get up there we follow our own route."

"Katie told me we have to climb a waterfall."

"It's not so much a climb as a scramble," he said, pausing a second as the server brought us more beers. "It's a few hundred feet up, and you'll be pulling yourself by rocks and roots, but we won't need ropes or anything."

Sue smiled. "Tell them about the helicopter."

Mark laughed. "Oh yeah, that. If you're not back within 24 hours of your declared time, they come get you."

"Sounds expensive," Katie said. She was right. When we returned home that afternoon, she researched the cost of a helicopter extract from high tundra in Newfoundland. It cost about as much as a small house. Undeterred, she called our insurance agent and explained our needs. After a week's wait, we were presented with a simple document to sign which eliminated any possibility of helicopter-induced bankruptcy in exchange for a one-time fee of $150. Now all we had to do was wait eight months.

■ ■ ■

Gros Morne in September is cool and humid. There was a slim chance of temperatures just above freezing overnight, but otherwise it was going to be long sleeves and jacket weather at worst. Katie and I each packed our own tent. We used to share a tent years ago, but that didn't last very long. At the end of a long day on the trail, one of us always smells and one of us always snores. And that one person is apparently me.

A typical three-season tent is usually made of rip-stop nylon or some other lightweight material. The inner portion is a thin mesh top with so-called "bathtub walls"—solid fabric extending from the ground to about shoulder height while seated, so rain or mud doesn't splash in. A separate rain fly over the mesh forms a protective dome to shed wind and rain, and also does a surprisingly good job of trapping body heat inside. A far cry from my old canvas shelter half.

A lightweight one-person tent is made of just enough material to hold one person and not much else. It's not meant as a luxurious home away from home; it's a nylon coffin meant to keep the elements off of you while you lie on the ground quietly. Mine was blue.

Mark suggested trekking poles and gaiters. We already had poles. I'd learned that lesson. But gaiters were a new concept. My ankle-high waterproof boots would not suffice. The likelihood of stepping in muck deeper than ankle height on this trip would be 100 percent, with multiple wet crossings, wide streams with no bridges—the whole place was, after all, a temporarily unfrozen tundra. Gaiters are basically a Gore-Tex sleeve for your shins that drape over the opening of your boot, preventing (most) water from getting in, and buckle under your heel. Quite effective, but also kind of ridiculous looking. Not that it mattered. When we reserved our dates, the rangers told us we would be the only ones up there.

Other than our tents and sleeping bags, we didn't plan to carry much else besides food and water. Fully loaded, Katie's pack and mine weighed around 30 pounds each, plus or minus a pound or two depending upon what luxuries I included, such as spare socks or extra chocolate.

Mark's kit weighed as much as two packs, because he actually carries two packs. In addition to his backpack, he also wears a frontpack with two DSLR camera bodies and multiple lenses and filters. His most powerful zoom is as long as my forearm and contains eight pounds of metal and glass. But when he uses it, you can count the flies on a caribou's butt from half a mile away, so there's that. Then there's the tripod, and the batteries: one for the light meter, plus a spare; one for each camera, plus a spare; plus rechargeable AAAs for the headlamp, Mark's ultraviolet water filter, and his GPS, which itself was a brick; bringing his total pack weight to over 60 pounds without water.

I whiled away the time obsessing over our contour map. The northwest corner of it was dominated by Western Brook Pond, a miles long, narrow, winding fjord. (Newfoundlanders call every body of water a pond. Western Brook is hundreds of square kilometers of clear blue water with tall, lapping waves. The same designation is given to a puddle you can step over.) The tip of it, right at the point, was where the ferry would drop us off. Outlining the pond were thick brown smears where the contour lines stacked one on top of the other—the vertical cliff faces I had seen on Katie's laptop.

Our map was oversized, sturdy, tear-resistant, waterproof, and expensive. The Long Range Traverse wasn't a very popular trek at the time, so the map needed to be specially ordered, and it took weeks to print and deliver. It was precious and it was our only copy, a fact I now recognize as the first entry on my short list of things I would go back and change if I could.

■ ■ ■

By the time Katie and I made it to St. John's airport that September, we were already tired. To get to St. John's (not to be confused with St. John without the "s", which is in New Brunswick) we'd had to fly in from Ontario, which we had flown into via Charlotte, which we had reached by flying out of Asheville, a 19-minute hop preceded by three hours on the runway. We had left our house 14 hours ago, and still had to drive 700 kilometers to the ferry before we could even think about hiking.

When Mark arrived, we helped him with his enormous bag and lugged our gear out to the car Katie had rented, a brand new maroon 2010 Dodge Charger with less than 100 miles on the odometer, premium sound system, and gray leather seats. "This was all they had," she said.

"We're going to destroy the interior in this thing," Mark said, climbing in. "At the very least we'll ruin the new car smell."

St John's is the capital and largest city in

Newfoundland, which is not to say that it's a large city at all, more of a fishing town that grew exponentially over the years. There are quaint houses, plenty of pubs, and incredible seafood. The music in the pubs is a peculiar blend of old time sea chanty mixed with a hint of bluegrass and a heavy dose of whiskey. The lyrics are usually about catching fish in nets and the girl that got away, or vice versa.

We stayed in a little place by the water, and awoke only slightly hungover. Driving west on Highway 1, the lone highway in Newfoundland, we soon lost radio reception, so Mark talked about the local flora and fauna. We could expect alpine vegetation and tuckamore, a thick tangle of low, stunted trees, he said. And plenty of moose. In fact, just as he said it, we passed one, wading knee-deep in a pond beside the road. Next to it was a sign that said *DILDO*. Of course we took the exit.

Parking at a pier in the tiny coastal fishing town, we stared down in wonder at the bluest water we'd ever seen. Back in the states, wooden pier posts are covered with seaweed and grime, sloshed by murky brown froth, usually with a paper cup floating nearby. These posts were obviously old and had a few barnacles, but the water was so clear I could see all the way to the bottom. I could even pick out the jellyfish hanging lazily in beams of sun.

It didn't take long for a few locals to come out and greet us. We learned that the town was named after an old sailing captain. Yes, Dildo came from a seaman.

One kind-eyed Dildoian warned us to be on the lookout when driving near the reedy parts. "Otherwise," he said, "ya might wind up with a moose on yer bonnet."

We thanked him and returned to the car, sniggering like schoolchildren. "Captain Dildo!"

■ ■ ■

Several radio-less hours later, we got to the visitor center at Gros Morne, just in time to take the test. First, a park ranger reviewed our four-day planned itinerary and route. "You get a 24-hour grace period, and then..." She whirled her finger over her head, mimicking a helicopter's blades.

"How will you find us?" Mark asked. "I mean, how would you find us, not that you'll need to."

"With this." She handed Katie our transponder, a small bit of metal the size, shape, and weight of an AA battery with a 10-inch flexible antenna protruding from one end. This locater beacon would tell the bird exactly where to land. "I don't need to tell you not to lose this," the ranger said.

Then we each had to show we were at least carrying a compass and could use it to point ourselves north or southwest when asked. Then she raised the difficulty a little, ordering us to point toward a precise azimuth: "Turn and face 247 degrees," she ordered. Still, this was basic compass stuff. The real skill would be knowing when and where out of all 360 degrees that 247 was the one you wanted.

That was the point of the written exam. We were given a map and a few pages of questions. "What is the name of the pond at the following coordinates?" "What is the distance and bearing between the two following features?" But we were prepared, and with me as the test-taking ringer, we aced the final. We were congratulating ourselves on a near-perfect score when the front door flung open and a lanky muscular couple walked in. They had just finished the Traverse and were looking for a ride back to their car, parked 20 miles back at the boat launch.

"Let's hit 'em up for beta," Mark said, and headed off to introduce himself. "Beta" was a term that had worked its way into Mark's vocabulary during his rock climbing days. It means getting the scoop from locals on where to go and what routes to take. Mark is an excellent source of new and exciting vocabulary.

The two introduced themselves as Theo and Nadine. Both were unusually tall and had muscular legs clad in gaiters from the knees down. His hair was unkempt and her arms looked like she'd done the whole thing walking on her hands.

"So, how was it?" I asked as we got in the car.

"Eet was eazee," said Theo, his intonation rising in typical French Canadian fashion. "We had some bad wezzair, but once we got to ze Long Range, eet was a highway."

The place with no trails was "a highway"?

But these two did have quads like tree trunks, and thousands of miles caked on their boots, whereas mine still had the little plastic thingy from the pricetag.

"How were the black flies?" Katie asked.

"Zey were not too bad. Nadine had to wear her net

for, what, half a day? But zey did not bozzer us."

As we continued to pelt him with questions, we learned that the terrain up there was a cross between the Andes, the Rockies, parts of Oregon, and a hint of the Alps, along with a dizzying array of other places none of us had ever been to, including the Moon. After this hike, they were immediately headed for Japan to do something called the Southern Alps. The two of them had pretty much circumnavigated the globe on foot.

"We hike too much, if zis is possible," Theo continued. "Zis was zee..." He paused, counting in his head. "Zee 54th night we have spent in a tent zees year."

That number stuck with me. 54. It was September, still the third quarter back in office land, and these two had already spent more nights in a tent that year than I had in vacation days for the next four years combined. I was inspired to know such a thing was possible. (When I finally hiked the Appalachian Trail, on my 54th night in my tent I thought of Theo and Nadine—who, by the way, considered the AT a "nice beginner hike.")

"Ah, look!" Theo said. "We are at zee parking lot! Whee!"

And with that, they thanked us and bounded off to their car, and I assume, something incredible.

. . .

The following morning, Sunday, we were standing in precisely the same spot. We left our maroon Dodge Charger placed at the visitor center where our journey would end and got a shuttle to the boat launch. "It's never the same hike twice," the driver told us. "At least not for me, and I've been up there a bunch, eh?"

Theo had just been lucky, he said. "There are plenty of highways up there, made by moose and caribou. Follow the wrong one and you'll be up there for a while. Have fun!"

We double-checked, then triple-checked our gear, and set out for the ferry dock. A friendly couple commented on our backpacks, and we explained how, unlike the other 72 passengers on our sightseeing boat, the three of us would jump off in the middle of the ride.

Looming in the distance were the soaring cliffs, which towered above choppy waters under a gray cloudy sky. Much of the path from the lot to the dock wound through bogs, with sturdy wooden boardwalks. The wind picked up and caught our packs like sails, forcing us to walk with a slight list to port. This was more than just annoying—my gaiters only protected me from the shins down, and those bogs looked neck-deep.

At the dock, we had an hour to snack and quadruple-check our gear, then were on our way up the ramp and onto the boat. After a safety briefing and the distribution of life vests, the engines puttered and we rocked out into the surging waves. Wherever I stood, I got splashed by spray, but I didn't mind. Every time we neared a cliff, I couldn't stop thinking, We're going to be up there soon.

Our little ferry churned and sputtered along, just a speck next to these massive rock walls. Their height would have still been dizzying were we merely standing still, rather than rocking about. Spouting from one of them was a waterfall I recognized from photos, known as Pissing Mare, that seemed to end in midair as the updraft turned it into mist and sent it back into the sky.

I grabbed Katie. "We're almost there!"

As the boat neared the turnaround point, we saw the waterfall we'd need to ascend far off in the distance at the back of a gorge. "Those of you with back country permits, grab your packs," announced the tour guide, and the other passengers looked at us as though we were crazy.

"It's going to be a touch-and-go," the tour guide told me. "We're not stopping, only slowing down."

He wasn't kidding. I spotted a platform of wood, a large pallet at best, secured to the shore by some posts. The captain aimed the vessel and killed the throttle. We were drifting, but fast.

And we were blocked. To my right, an old lady stood with her eye pressed firmly to the view port of her digital camera, taking a video of another spectacular waterfall and oblivious to our presence.

"Marge, move!" her husband scolded. "These folks need to get off."

"Just a minute," she said.

"Marge, they don't have a minute!"

The dock loomed larger. I cleared my throat, which is about as aggressive as I like to get when dealing with strangers.

Her husband yelled, "MARGE!"

"Oh come on!" she shot back.

The captain's voice came over the speaker. "Okay, folks, we're here!"

I rotated my body slightly counterclockwise, admittedly causing my pack to gently make contact with her arm, though I contend that it was a rogue wave that knocked her aside, not me. Then with Marge out of the way, and only seconds to make the leap, I hopped onto the wooden platform and my companions joined me.

We turned around to watch the ferry already speeding off, engines churning, until the sound of it was drowned out by the rush of waterfalls in the gorge. We stayed there for a while, silently quintuple-checking our gear, though if we'd forgotten anything it was now too late. Retreat was impossible. The only way home was forward. Which was behind us.

Mark spoke up. "It's 2:00 now, and the sun goes down around 7:30. Ready?"

It takes seasoned hikers five to seven hours to make it to the top of our destination waterfall, which we could hear but not see. Directly between us and the 700-foot near-vertical climb was a 4-kilometer tangle of thick brush, bugs, and giant rocks. We faced east and stepped off.

Not only was there no path, but when Mark and Katie were only a few steps ahead of me, they would completely disappear, hidden by ferns taller than me and moss-covered boulders leaning at every angle.

The stream flowing past us to Western Brook Pond was fed by at least three waterfalls we could see and about three more we could only hear. Nature was playing a water symphony for us, but I could hear none of it over the discordant jam session buzzing and crawling on my bug net.

Mark, despite practically living in the outdoors, somehow has never developed a proper "outside voice." Despite his 65-pound packs, he scampered easily over the wet rocks and wide streams, stopping to call back to us something inaudible before scampering off again.

Katie was able to keep up with him enough to relay messages from the front of our motley parade to the back.

"What did he say?" I yelled to her after Mark gave another indistinguishable shout.

"I think he's breaking out the GPS."

Already? I thought. *We just got here.*

CHAPTER 12
DEAD RECKONING

GETTING FROM THE FERRY drop off to the base of the waterfall wasn't so much a navigational challenge as it was an exercise in route finding. It was easy to see where we wanted to be, but rather hard to get there.

The canyon walls to our left and right prevented straying too far from our desired path, but the floor of the gorge was by no means level. We had to climb over numerous mounds, boulders, and fallen logs. Visibility was limited by the thick vegetation and the twisting path. We were being funneled into a point, but the gorge was not a straight line, and even climbing atop a high rock or the one tree strong enough to hold me, line of sight was a few dozen meters at best.

Stay right of the falls. That was our mantra as we trudged forward. One might think that simply staying to the right of the stream would guarantee this, but none of the trip reports had mentioned there were multiple streams, and multiple falls feeding them.

"Marco!"

"Polo!" This time it was Mark who replied. He and

Katie had climbed up a mossy rock to get a better view. "I think we're almost there," he told me when I reached the top.

"I agree, but can we get there from here?"

"I think so. I'll scout ahead." He climbed down the other side. I rested beside Katie, removing my pack as I plopped onto the moss. I was thirsty, but dared not remove my head net. So many black flies were buzzing around my head, they were tricking me into thinking I was seeing spots and about to pass out. I fed the bite valve of my Camelbak under the elastic and took a long, refreshing sip. "I hope we don't have to turn around again," I said.

Three times we'd had to backtrack already. Once after we thought we could hike up and over something only to find it was actually a dangerous drop. Another time when we'd followed a path that continued to shrink until our only option was to crawl. Most recently, I'd thought we were at the falls, only to discover that I'd led us to an impossible wet climb up one of the side walls.

Our map was shoved into one of my cargo pockets. Even folded multiple times, it was still too bulky to fit fully, and the corner stuck out. I had already developed the habit of touching it often to make sure it was still there. Just as I was about to unfold it and have another look, Mark said something inaudible from up ahead. I gave Katie a quizzical look.

"That almost sounded like 'I found it,'" she said, and went ahead to verify, disappearing into the green mess. A moment later she called back, "We got it!"

■   ■   ■

Looking up from the base of the falls, the back of the gorge was a slick rock wall, nearly vertical and gleaming wet from the high stream spilling over its top. I was surprised by how narrow the falls were. Now I understood why we couldn't see it, despite having heard it for so long. To its left, all the way from where we stood to the limit of our vision, was sheer and vertical. Nothing to grab or step on. The wall to the right wasn't much better—not completely vertical, but close. Its steep slope was covered in tuckamore.

"Are you sure this is it?" I asked.

Mark frowned. "It has to be. This looks like the end of the line."

Katie moved in for a closer look. "I think we're going to have to pull ourselves up the tuck." She was right.

The small trees grew almost horizontally as they clung to the rock, which meant we could use their trunks as a makeshift ladder, stepping from one trunk to the next. Unfortunately, they were so closely packed that securing a foothold still left us having to twist our bodies into bizarre and unpleasant contortions. On several occasions the root I grabbed pulled free, leaving me holding the thing I'd hoped would hold me.

We scraped our fingers on the rock and skinned our hands raw on the tough bark as we continued to pull ourselves up the side of the falls. About halfway up I noticed that the bugs weren't following us. Both the net and my windbreaker were unnecessary, and both were collecting the perspiration from my efforts. But there was no way to take off my pack and stow gear mid-climb, so I squinted against the stinging sweat and pulled myself up to the next trunk.

Leaves and branches in my face blocked most of my view, and the only clues that I was nearing the top were the patches of gray sky above and the lack of grunting and cursing coming from my companions. The slope became more forgiving and the little bits of gray grew larger and larger, until I at last emerged into a clearing atop a slanted rock face. Katie was lounging by the rushing stream that fed our unnamed waterfall, while Mark knelt with a big lens up to his eye, clicking furiously, shooting everything.

Silently, I dropped my pack and turned around to face the view. "Oh my god," I said, then pulled off my bug net and collapsed.

No photo could have prepared me. The bottom half of the gorge made a lush V, so green it was almost black. Stone walls jutted craggy and gray out of the verdant mess. The tip of the pond reflected an overcast silver sky, and if I squinted, I could make out the tiny wooden pier where we'd leapt off the boat. Pissing Mare was doing its thing, sending a fine mist upward. The whole thing looked like a miles-long zigzagging crack in the earth, overflowing with water and trees. As if on cue, a real crack appeared, this one in the sky. The clouds parted just enough to allow a few crepuscular rays to shine down onto the valley, briefly spotlighting it with patches of gold as we watched the sun set over the gorge we'd just climbed.

Our shirts were wet with the sweat from the climb,

and the wind at the top was cool and steady. At first this was refreshing, but it quickly became a bit uncomfortable. We were famished, and we still had to find a place to spend the rapidly approaching night.

We ascended for about 20 minutes, constantly looking back over our shoulders as our view of the gorge improved with each step. Eventually we came to a large bowl-shaped area the size of a football stadium, and we were finally truly at the top.

Hundreds of oddly shaped puddles were connected by meandering streams, filled with clear water tinged copper by tannins from decaying vegetation. The flattest, driest spots still had the squishy feel of a freshly watered lawn. I laid out my tarp, and while I was fishing my tent out of my pack, the wind lifted the tarp and wrapped it around my legs. It took a combination of tent poles and rocks to subdue the thing, and getting the actual tent set up was an exercise in flapping frustration as well.

We prepared a quick meal of dehydrated noodles and some cheese, and devoured it by the light of our headlamps. Then we switched them off and gawked for a while at the Milky Way. Here, much closer to the North Pole than I'm used to being, the constellations were all shifted and too close to the horizon. It was disorienting and made me feel the distance from home. Then, exhausted, we crawled into our tents and were soon asleep.

■ ■ ■

I awoke to the sound of three zippers: Katie getting out

of her sleeping bag, opening her tent door, and then the rain fly. She walked toward Mark's tent and I could tell from their conversation that he had already been up for an hour taking pictures. It was cold, but I looked forward to stepping out because I knew the view was incredible.

Swallowing what would be the first of many Advil, I unfolded myself, stepped into my Crocs and turned toward the gorge. "Not a bad place to wake up, eh?" I shouted.

We had breakfast, and while Katie filtered some water for all of us, Mark and I planned our route for the day. This was a few years before smart phones, and Mark, being a gear junkie, had a vintage GPS unit, one of the first to be commercially available. It had a tiny screen and took a few minutes to boot up.

"Okay, in a minute it'll figure out where we are," Mark said. "Just has to get satellites first."

"Cool. While we're waiting, we're here," I pointed to our location on the topo, at the summit of the pointy smear of relief lines representing the gorge. "It took us about five hours to get from the dock to where we are now, and if we can keep the same pace, we should make it to Mark's Pond and maybe even Harding's."

The three potential campsites to our south were Little Island Pond, Mark's Pond, and Harding's Pond, though the term "campsite" is used here rather loosely. The Canadian National Park Service had constructed a bunch of 10'x10' raised wooden platforms, each about six inches tall, and dropped them in groups of three from a helicopter at various points along the hiking routes from the top of the waterfall to the base of Gros Morne

Mountain. The platforms provide no shelter at all, and merely exist to prevent having to put your tent directly on the ground. This is partially for hikers' comfort, but mostly to protect the fragile landscape.

Mark's GPS was fully operational now. A little blip on the screen was us, and we were zoomed in so far that I could tell we were looking at contours, but not which ones. "The numbers are what really matters," Mark explained. "Here's our latitude and longitude, which we can use to find ourselves on the map. I've already programmed in the coordinates for the sites we want. Okay, look!"

A small red arrow pointed the way, along with the corresponding desired compass angle, our azimuth.

"What if something gets in our way?"

"We go around it and check again."

This would get us out in an emergency, but if we had to keep doing it all day we'd never get anywhere, and we'd probably drain the batteries. Mark's GPS was old school tech, but I preferred older school: good old map and compass.

We were now facing our first navigational challenge. We were on a giant plateau, with no more big climbs but still plenty of obstacles. The lack of big climbs meant a lack of easily identifiable mountains. Stretched out before us lay a collection of irregular mounds and more ponds than I could count. I tried to pick a pond with a memorable shape and locate its twin on the map, using dead reckoning so I wouldn't even need my compass.

"Once we're over the ridge to our south, we should be able to make this large unnamed pond, and once we get to the south of that, we should see Little Island Pond. Should be easy, right?"

"Gravy," Mark said.

I ran my plan past Katie, who was returning with our water supply. "I got us to Newfoundland," she said. "I'm done making decisions. I'm here to relax. You boys get us out."

· · ·

The previous day's hike had been claustrophobic; sheer cliff walls to our left and right closed in on us as we progressed, an effect amplified by the nets we wore on our heads. What we saw from the top of this ridge was the exact opposite of that. We were met with a vast expanse of green, peppered with rocks of all sizes. The horizon was impossibly distant, and right in the center of it all was a giant pond. How something so huge could lack a name boggled us, but one thing was certain: We were in the right place. Before us was a bird's-eye view corresponding exactly with our desired location on the map. Little did we know, it was the last time we'd enjoy such navigational luxury.

I could not contain myself. "Holy shit! Would you look at that!"

"Ah yes, eet is zhust like a highway," Mark said.

Because the Long Range Traverse is tundra, the ground only ever exists in one of two possible conditions: frozen solid or soggy. Now it felt like a high altitude swamp without reptiles or the right trees. Anything that looked grassy had a 50 percent chance of actually being shin deep muck. The glaciers that once covered the area had deposited rocks they carried from many miles away, known as erratics because of their dissimilarity to the local terrain. Anvil-shaped boulders dotted the marshy fields, connected by stands of tuckamore and streams the color of weak tea.

Gradually, we turned our focus from the horizon to the ground directly in front of us. There were so many rocks, puddles, and tripping hazards that long-range planning was guesswork anyway. Mark, the most surefooted of us, set off down the slope and we followed. As we reached the bottom of the ridge, just to the right of the unnamed pond, a curious thing happened. We found a trail, complete with the boot prints of previous hikers.

"*This* must be the highway," Katie said.

It seemed to have as many hoof prints as boot prints, so we checked the map to make sure it wasn't one of the misleading game trails we had read about. Reassured, we followed it south for about an hour, and arrived at Little Island Pond well before lunchtime. We were making good time and decided to try pushing past our planned campsite at Mark's Pond and to spend the night at Harding's Pond instead. Thick fog was in tomorrow's forecast, so stretching today would give us some leeway if we were socked in.

We continued along the path, and I started to regret mocking Theo's highway observation. "I thought there wasn't supposed to be a trail up here."

"There isn't a marked trail," Katie clarified.

Midstride, she stopped, then turned around and raised her hands to the side of her head, thumbs at her temples, fingers splayed out. Antlers! She'd spotted a moose!

It was the first wild moose of the hike, and I was thrilled. (The one we'd seen from the moving car didn't really count.) The three of us stopped and gawked, while the moose watched us. She was a cow; a bull to her right had just ducked into the tuckamore, so I missed him.

We continued our southward progress past Little Island Pond, following the path, and frequently checking our position. The ground flattened considerably, which would ordinarily come as a tremendous relief to any hiker. But in the tundra during summer, flat equals wet. The path became increasingly tricky to follow, and as previous hikers and moose had veered off, it widened and sometimes vanished altogether. Skirting along a chain of small ponds to our left, we eventually came to the large creek that feeds into Mark's Pond and followed it for a bit, looking for a crossing that wouldn't get our feet soaked. Gaiters and boots had kept my socks dry so far, and I hoped to maintain that for as long as possible.

The mud deepened as the trail wound in and out of the tuckamore, limiting our view to a few meters in any direction. I was getting a little claustrophobic again. Mark decided to scout ahead, so we waited, Katie ahead of me in her usual spot in the middle of our parade. It had been about 20 minutes since our last stop, so I decided to verify our position while we waited for Mark to report back. I reached into the map pocket—and felt nothing.

Then nothing was replaced by adrenaline. My cheeks flushed and the back of my neck began to sweat. I frantically patted every pocket I could reach, already knowing better.

"Shit," I finally said aloud.

Katie turned back to me. "What?"

"I lost the map."

CHAPTER 13
PUDDLE JUMPING

We might get to ride in a helicopter, I considered as I dropped my gear with Katie and backtracked to look for the missing map. It had been about 20 minutes since our most recent stop, which was the last time I could recall seeing it. Now it would either be lying quietly back where I'd left it or blowing across the tundra, never to be seen again.

When you're lost, they tell you to stay put. We still had two more days before anyone would even begin thinking about us, and I was not looking forward to setting up camp at that stream crossing. The only thing soggier than the ground would be Mark and Katie's mood. I'd ribbed him earlier about how his technology was unreliable. The ability to read a map only works if you actually *have* the damn thing.

At one particular bend, the "highway" widened like the extra lanes at a toll booth. The toll: stepping through an expansive pit of brown glop, shallower at the edges up against the tuckamore, where past travelers had skirted the deeper muck at the center. Deep glop or shallow muck. I'd remembered what a hassle it was to cross this the first time, and dreaded the idea of negotiating it twice more. As before, I picked strenuous rather than messy, grabbing the stunted pines for support as I squirmed through at the edges.

Ordinarily my mind would have wandered—the sky was bright blue with only a few clouds, and I could hear the big lazy stream now to my right. The twisting path forced my attention downward, and it's a good thing, because as I approached the next wide patch of muck I was greeted by a satisfying white rectangle resting just to the left of the path. I ran straight through the deepest part of the sludge, snatched the dear thing up, and kissed it, mud be damned.

Thank god, I thought, I'm not a dumb ass! I hadn't stupidly left the map on the ground where we'd last used it. As we wriggled through the tuck around this mini bog, one of the many grabby branches must have caught the corner of the map and yanked it out.

When I returned, Katie was resting nearby. "Did you find it?" she asked excitedly.

Earlier in the day, Mark and I had had a race to see who could find our location the quickest. When the map won, I had waved it above my head like a battle standard. As I showed it to Katie this time, it felt more like the white rag of surrender. I reassured her that we were okay because I had been in the habit of checking to be sure I still had it by patting my pocket every so often, a habit which I'd begun faithfully practicing almost exactly one minute ago.

"Put it in my pack," she flatly ordered.

"Did Mark find a place to cross the creek?"

"Yep. He's up there right now waiting for us." She cupped her hands and yelled, "He found it!" and bounded into the tuck.

Mark's reply was something inaudible from up ahead.

"Cool," I said to no one. "I'll just put on my pack again and be right there." I grabbed my gear, glad to be on the move again, adjusted my straps, and stepped directly into a shin-deep pool of muck.

■   ■   ■

Compass work for this next leg would be simple. *Go south.* It is worth noting however, that south isn't always south. You probably recall from science class that compasses work because the Earth is a giant magnet. But there's a fun twist which is often revealed when you take a land navigation course. Our planet's molten core is not a perfect sphere, which throws off the field a little. On top of that, there is a massive iron ore deposit beneath Canada. It's a big enough chunk of metal to affect compasses as far away as Florida. Up in Newfoundland the needle is pulled 24 degrees to the left, enough to skew you a half mile off target for each hour of travel.

Fortunately, every good topo map makes note of this discrepancy, which is specific to your region and is listed as the angle of declination. Every good compass comes with a tiny adjustment screw that compensates for the effect by rotating your needle in the opposite direction, "zeroing" it and eliminating the need for you to do math on the march.

But because the highland is peppered with hundreds upon hundreds of pools, ponds, lakes, streams, puddles, and creeks, we could never travel in a straight line for more than a minute. Each short-term goal—say a rock or a tree, something close enough to see and easily point to—required a zigzag path and twice the anticipated time because of all the squishy bits.

Our aversion to the squishy bits was motivated by our desire to stay dry, and we were succeeding too, at least from the knees up. We also were being careful not to become stuck. Once, Mark's entire leg had vanished into a slimy crevasse concealed by what appeared to be a solid path of mossy dirt.

One other environmental condition slowing us down significantly was the sheer beauty of it all. Tuckamore isn't very tall, so no overhead canopy of trees shielded us from the sky or the gentle breeze. The dark green horizon was mostly flat, but not unbroken. Rather than rolling mountains, the landscape before us was a jumble of mini plateaus separated by tricky gorges, like smaller scale models of the waterfall gorge we'd climbed to get up here.

The squishy bits held our attention as tightly as they gripped our feet. Strange plants and flowers grew there, including brightly colored death traps called pitcher plants. Their long red and green stalks resemble a vase, which fills up with a sweet-smelling nectar and eventually, the bodies of any thirsty insects unlucky enough to try drinking the stuff. The pitcher is lined with sharp downward-facing barbs to hinder their escape as the struggling prey slowly dissolve. Really a lovely plant though. I use something similar to keep the fruit flies away from my bananas in the summer.

Katie was beginning to regret keeping the map in her pack. Mark and I had started announcing our need for a location check by calling out, "Oh, map wench!"

As we neared the top of the ridge from which Harding's Pond should be visible, a sight completely unexpected caught my eye.

"What the hell is that?"

It was obviously a house, far off. But two days into our trek, having seen very few living things and having heard no sounds to indicate civilization of any kind, the sight of a green, two-story, well maintained house complete with chimneys and a wraparound porch was like encountering an elephant at a bus stop.

"That's got to be the ranger cabin," Katie explained. "If we can see it, we're on the right track. We're not supposed to walk toward it though, since our route is in the opposite direction."

As we descended the ridge, our view of the cabin improved. It was obviously unoccupied and we could now see a pair of boats overturned nearby. I wondered how the rangers got there. Helicopter, probably.

At the base of the ridge, we put the ranger station well behind us and enjoyed a good long stretch of the flattest land we'd been on that day. With the pond to our left, we squished our way to the wooden platforms at Harding's Pond, Mark taking the first, Katie the second, and I the third, all the way at the western edge. They would be our home for the night: a roughly 10-foot square of planks with no overhead shelter whatsoever, just eye hooks at the corners for tying down tents or tarps.

We ate at my platform, scanned the map, and discussed our route for the following day. If we continued at our current pace, we would have time to scale Gros Morne Mountain on the last morning, followed by what appeared on the map to be a gentle stroll back to the car. Black cliffs at the far shore reflected perfectly in the pond, except when small fish or frogs broke its mirror surface. As dusk approached, I was thrilled to imagine how spectacular this scene would appear at sunrise.

Basking in optimism and endorphins, we retreated to our tents. I swallowed a pair of Advil and read a few chapters of *Road Fever* by Tim Cahill, while listening to the waves lap at the shore. A gentle breeze found its way under the rain fly. A nearby tiny waterfall shushed my thoughts and gradually I shut my eyes.

■ ■ ■

In my dream, the sound of the tiny waterfall became road noise from a nearby highway—one not made of mud. Eventually, the sound of rushing water brought on a different sensation.

If you have never had the pleasure of subsisting on mostly dehydrated food for several days, there is something you may not have considered. Between the cooking, eating, and drinking during a single dinner, you easily ingest two liters of water. The sponge-like nature of the rations makes them absorb anything you drink. A few hours later, all that liquid wants out at once.

The simple act of sitting up shot a bright bolt of urgency through my lower parts. Now shivering, both from the cold and the fight I was losing against my bladder, I squirmed, slid, and stood from my tent, stepped into my Crocs, and relieved myself a few steps away from my platform.

Backcountry etiquette dictates that you make waste at least 150 yards from where you sleep and eat, but I not only forgave myself the transgression, but was impressed to have made it as many steps as I had.

When finished, I wobbled the few steps back to my tent, rummaged through the stuff sack I use as a pillow, and put on an extra layer of clothing before zipping back into my bag. I briefly considered a hat, then drifted off once again to the sound of wind and waterfalls.

When I next opened my eyes, it was daylight. A fine layer of backlit drops coated the outside of my rain fly. I'd not heard it rain; it was a barely perceptible mist, just enough to make me wonder whether I had remembered to pull my boots under the fly. I had. However, my wet socks which I'd hung on some branch to dry would now be wetter than they had been when I'd removed them.

Exiting the tent was way more complicated than it had been the previous morning. My legs were super stiff, and I was developing a bruise on my lower spine from where my pack weight rested. I wrung out my socks, and confirmed that placing my boots inside the rain fly had failed to dry them. Despite the vast amounts of water which had passed through my system the previous night, I felt dehydrated. I was hungry. I was cold. And somehow I was actually quite happy.

Mark obviously had been up long before me and was intently focusing on one particular knob on his tripod. "Interesting light this morning. It keeps changing…too rapidly for a good panorama." He pointed out that the clouds were moving at right angles to one other. A band of bright white mist was crashing into the path of a black mass directly above us. "I've never seen the sky do that before, and it looks like the darker ones are headed our way. I'm getting some good shots though."

"Oh man, that really is creepy," I said, and shivered a bit. "How are your boots?"

"They're about the only dry part of me right now."

We had our usual breakfast of cold blueberry granola with dehydrated cream. Once again we checked the map and reviewed the plan for the day. We'd read back at the boat launch that precipitation and windy conditions were predicted for today. Not sure how long it would last or whether it would worsen, we decided to travel as far as possible while we could still see. The black clouds headed our way could bring rain or fog that would pin us down.

Another full day of hiking would get us through something ominously named the Middle Barrens and then past Green Island Pond, then west for a while to the edge of the gorge formed by Ten Mile Pond, another zigzagging smear of stacked relief lines on the map indicating a 1,000-foot drop into the blue at the bottom. This was a true navigational no-brainer: arrive at the giant cliff, stop, turn left. If we could follow that clifftop for a couple hours, we would reach our final steep descent to the last official campsite at Ferry Gulch.

Katie's research told us this final descent would be clearly marked by cairns—obvious piles of rocks stacked by hikers from years past. Ferry Gulch and the final set of platforms would await us at the base of Gros Morne Mountain, a stark trapezoid of rock and rubble. Also known as "Big Baby" and "The Big Lonely," this phenomenal pile of scree had dominated the horizon while we were making our initial preparations, and if we could rest at its foot on our final night, the last day of our hike would take us up and over the beast.

I could only imagine how incredible it would feel to stand on the top of that massive mound, surveying craggy desolation behind us, an ocean before us. Somewhere between the water and us, but still miles ahead, would be the lonely parking lot where salvation awaited in the form of a maroon Dodge Charger, sitting in silence at the rate of 40 dollars Canadian a day.

With bellies full, and confident that we were about to achieve a Theo-like feat of wilderness conquest, we happily marched along the Highway. The low mist thickened around us as the high clouds to our right broke. With half the sky gently drizzling and the other half shooting beams of sun over the distant hills, a giant rainbow appeared. Surely this was a good omen!

For nearly an hour, the rainbow stayed to our right. We were almost two hours out of camp before the temperature warmed enough for us to stop and remove our raincoats. It was about then that Mark confirmed via GPS that we were way off course.

CHAPTER 14
THE MIDDLE BARRENS: DESTROYER OF PLANS

WITH AN EXCELLENT map, three compasses, and a GPS, we still had managed to get lost. This happens a lot on the Long Range Traverse. Trails that seem useful are in reality made by creatures that live in the wilderness and have no plans to leave it. To follow them almost assuredly guarantees the same fate.

We had grown complacent and had neglected to ascend a ridge line on our right about an hour earlier, instead choosing to "gravity hike" by following the path of least resistance. Now it was far steeper, and we needed to find a way up.

After deciding against backtracking, we picked out a path through the tuckamore and started to scramble up the grade through the marsh, muck, rocks, and impassible thick vegetation, often veering as much as 50 yards off course just to gain about ten feet of altitude.

Each time we arrived at what appeared to be the top of the ridge, a slightly higher and more difficult ridge arose beyond it. Each time we thought we were at the last plateau, another loomed. Each time we believed we had a straight shot to our goal, the terrain threw some hidden obstacle at us, forcing yet another squishy uphill detour. We'd somehow gone from pointing excitedly up and to our right, to pointing dejectedly up and to our left. And eventually behind us.

We were stopping often to check our position and bearing. Katie somehow stopped seeing the humor in my constantly summoning her as "map wench" and gave the map to Mark. He'd fire up the GPS, sacrificing precious battery life while I'd point my compass at some distant peak. "These four ponds," I'd say, pointing at the map, "should be…here," indicating the other side of some treacherous slope. Mark would concur. Katie remained silent.

"Dude, is she alright?" Mark asked me privately. "Should I ask her how she is?"

"It's best not to," I replied. Ordinarily, silence from one's wife might be a sign that she is upset. With Katie, however, I believe her refusal to speak during situations like this reflects her unswerving dedication to the mission. When decisions need to be made in the wilderness, she probably thinks that to introduce an additional conflicting opinion will create a "too many cooks in the kitchen" problem, and that it's best to loyally support the team.

Or at least I assume that's why she's quiet. She won't say.

. . .

"Not that anyone's counting," Mark said during one particularly twisted attempt to crest the ridge, "but we've had to turn around seven times."

"Total, or just today?"

The tiniest canyon ever blocked our path, six inches wide and two feet deep, with a mere trickle running at the bottom. "Just once yesterday," Mark answered, hopping over it. "Seven today."

Katie continued to say nothing.

I spotted a narrow pass through more tuck which wound back and forth for about 50 feet before eventually emerging into what appeared to be a small clearing. We passed through the narrow opening and in moments came to a natural rock stair, each rise about five feet. I tossed my trekking poles ahead, grabbed a sturdy root and hoisted myself up. From this new vantage I could see Mark resting in the small clearing. I turned back to Katie.

"Can I get a hand?" she asked. I braced myself with one hand on a narrow trunk and extended my other for her. As she pulled herself up, I saw (and heard) her knee strike a sharp corner on the rock. I winced on her behalf, but she was in the zone, either not noticing the pain or simply past caring.

I turned and caught up with Mark, who was crouched near a flattened pile of moss.

"How's Katie?" he asked.

"Whatever you do, don't ask her."

The moss had obviously been squashed by something very large. Maybe even multiple somethings.

The area was conspicuously devoid of the blueberries we'd become accustomed to snacking upon. Surveying the scene, we saw a large set of antlers quickly—and surprisingly silently—dashing behind the bush just a few feet away.

He was a hefty bull, easily seven feet at the shoulder, and moved with startling grace through thick trees and bushes we would have zero chance of negotiating. We were in his house, and we were extremely lucky that it was not currently rutting season. He tolerated us, occasionally shooting an annoyed look as he munched whatever green he could reach.

After about ten minutes of marveling at this close encounter, we continued on, occasionally looking back to confirm that we weren't about to get charged. The bull continued his munching, having seemingly already forgotten us. We were so excited to see this beautiful creature that we almost failed to notice that we were back on the Highway.

▪ ▪ ▪

We confirmed our location. Then we double checked, and at my insistence we triple checked. We were right back where we needed to be, so comfortably we marched on.

There was no way in hell we were going to make it all the way to Ferry Gulch by sunset, and now would probably have to stop at Green Island, having added an unintended 4-hour loop prior to our moose sighting. Fortunately, our overall plan allowed for that kind of flexibility; we had built in some "just in case" time and it was definitely getting used.

I used the map to find the angle from us to Green Island Pond and shot an azimuth toward our desired location. It lined up with a distant pyramid-shaped mountain on the horizon, the longest line of sight since we started. It was miles beyond the pond, but if we could focus on that pyramid we'd eventually walk right into the pond.

After heading towards the mountain for a while, once again we encountered a marshy area that forced us to spread out. Like Marines in a rice paddy, we were on patrol, spread out and tiptoeing in the same direction.

"Marco!" It was Katie.

Since I was farthest ahead, I stopped and replied. "Polo!" A moment passed and Mark muttered something inaudible. Katie answered him, and he began walking in the direction from which we'd just come.

"What did he say?" I shouted to Katie.

"He lost the map."

I removed my pack and sat on a rock. "Well…I guess we live here now!"

. . .

I felt old as I creaked down onto the rock. A sudden breeze chilled my sweaty back, making me shiver as I reached into my pocket for a snack. I was hungry, tired, cold, and once again we were without a map.

When Katie got to me, I was zoned out and staring silently at the pyramid-shaped silhouette on the far horizon.

"What do you make of this?" she asked.

"I think we'll be fine," I laughed. "We always are."

We had the GPS, and we had our collective memory of the map, which we'd been studying for weeks and staring at every five minutes for the past three days.

We sat for a few minutes talking about the plan, which had changed so much since we set out that morning. We were both tired, not just physically.

"I think we need to be more over that way," Katie said, pointing to our left. My navigation technique had lapsed into Marine mode: shoot an azimuth on a distant obvious target and then walk straight toward it for as long as possible. If something gets in your way, go through it or over it. This works just fine when trying to traverse relatively flat terrain, but to attempt that method in the high tundra was a sure sign of exhaustion, frustration, or both. I collected my thoughts and pulled in my gaze from the dark triangle miles away and allowed my eyes to rest on the steep muddy slope a few short steps ahead.

I responded with the phrase every wife loves most to hear from her husband: "I think you're right."

Katie had every reason to say, "I told you so," but didn't. After all, she was the only member of our party to not lose the map so far. Instead, she showed me the hint of a smile and just then we were interrupted.

From somewhere behind us, Mark cried out.

"WOOOOOOOOOOO!"

"I believe that's the first thing I've heard and understood from Mark at a distance of greater than five feet."

Moments later he came bounding down to where we sat, grinning and clutching a wet, crumpled map. "I thought for sure we were screwed this time," he said. "I don't remember when I dropped it, but it was pretty easy to spot. It's the only big white square thing up here. It was moving pretty quick when I caught it, too."

The breeze had picked up significantly, especially on the high ground. I could easily picture the map tumbling along the hilltop, bouncing across the landscape from puddle to puddle, snagging on sticks, with Mark running behind it, arms outstretched.

As Katie suggested, the three of us moved about 50 meters to our left, Mark found a path down the muddy slope before us, and we pressed on. Our hike gradually became a trudge. The wind picked up, and conversation lagged. It took us nearly an hour to cross the valley, and before we made it to the top of the other side we'd traveled our greatest distance without talking.

When we crested the ridge, we remained silent. But now this speechlessness had an entirely new meaning: We could see the finish line.

Looming ominously ahead of us was the gray trapezoidal head of the Big Baby, Gros Morne. Barely perceptible as a blue flat haze behind it was the ocean. The ridge we'd just crested opened onto a great plateau, half a mile wide and peppered with glacial erratics, pools, and berry bushes. It was the biggest flat surface we'd seen for days, and the absence of vertical obstructions immediately called attention to the graying sky.

• • •

"Does anyone mind if we stop for a while and I set up the tripod?" Mark asked.

"Hell no!" Katie answered. "We wish you would!"

The unexpected change of scenery and the sight of our goal had definitely boosted the mood of our group. We quickly forgot that we'd spent the morning wandering directionless. We felt so energized, we even considered pressing on all the way to Ferry Gulch as we'd originally planned. It was at the base of Gros Morne, after all, and hell, there it was! You could almost touch it.

After an easy hour of standing, posing, munching, and reveling, we pressed on. After we crossed the plateau we were on, we still had to descend to Green Island Pond. We'd read that this descent would be the second-most difficult of the trip, and when we reached it an hour later, we had a hard time imagining what the number one would be like.

Green Island Pond's camping area was easily visible from a distance. It was the familiar green square of the privy thrones we'd come to know and love, sitting atop a lone mound overlooking the three wooden platforms which would be our home for the night. Just behind those was the pond, really just a wide spot in a stream, but very wide indeed and clearly flowing. We were about half a mile away and 200 feet above—50 of which would be a slick and tricky drop.

Standing at the edge, we could see the erosion from

previous hikers. They all obviously had zigzagged for about the first ten feet, and gauging from the torn roots and tangled branches, they had all found various ways to scale to the bottom. Mark went first. After about five minutes of scrambling, and tossing his pack from the halfway point, he reached the base. Katie and I followed, threw our packs and poles from the same point, and carefully used the exposed roots to lower ourselves. "Well, we're definitely not turning back now," Katie joked. No, we definitely were not.

It never felt so good to stop walking as when we reached the platforms at Green Island Pond. Katie and I immediately took off our wet boots and socks; Mark's were still mysteriously dry. The clouds we'd experienced on the plateau had broken or remained behind, and we all collapsed on our backs to soak in the sun. The gentle sound of the waterfalls and rapids that fed the creek combined with the warm rays to almost soothe us to sleep. Then, immediately, thousands of black flies descended on our faces.

"Good lord!" I shouted, rummaging for my bug hat. "I thought we left these bastards long behind!"

"It must be because we're so low now, and near the water," Mark replied, digging for his own cover.

I sprayed Deet on my hands and bare feet, and lay back down. It hurt to move. "Guys, I'm not even going to bother setting up my tent. I'm too tired to move, and it looks like it's going to be nice from here on out."

Sighing, arms and legs sprawled, I lifted my chin to my chest, opened one eye, and saw that Katie had nearly finished assembling her tent.

"How did you… How the…"

I let my head fall back to the platform.

Mark took pictures for about an hour, then we ate dinner and engaged in our nightly ritual of obsessing over the map.

Tomorrow morning would consist of hopping over a few relatively small hills, while gradually increasing our altitude until we would be at the same level as our earlier plateau. From there, we would skirt along the edge of a cliff before encountering the number one most treacherous descent of the trip and arriving at Ferry Gulch at the base of Gros Morne. We could leave most of our gear there while we scaled Gros Morne, then take a well-marked, well-worn trail back to the car. And food. And showers. And a bed. Speaking of which...

The sun was still shining when I finally pitched my tent, and shortly after that, I was deep asleep.

CHAPTER 15
THE BIG LONELY

A REPEATING GENTLE SLAP on my shoulder stirred me partially awake. Zipped to my chin, and with my arms snug inside my sleeping bag, I struggled briefly to turn and face my assailant. Blinking in the dark, I could see nothing. Now the slap hit me in the face, accompanied by a gust of cold air. Not one of my fellow campers, but part of my tent. One of my ties must have come undone, and some loose material was flapping in the breeze.

I unzipped and reached out to grope for the unsecured guy line, but what my hand found was as tight as a banjo string. My conscious mind rose up a bit more from the depths of sleep to assess the situation. Everything was secure. The wind was blowing under the rain fly and pushing the leeward wall of the tent against me. It was strong and it was cold.

Realizing that there was nothing more I could do, I decided to go back to sleep. First, though, I left the relative warmth of my bag just long enough to put on an extra shirt and my long johns. Then I wiggled back in, zipped up to my chin again, and closed my eyes. I think I lay for about an hour as my tent rocked like a hammock before I eventually dipped back down into fitful slumber. The last sound I remember was the gentle patter of sideways rain.

The following morning I awoke cold, stiff, and definitely not rested. I could hear some kind of motion coming from the direction of Mark's tent. "Good morning!" I called, still completely shrouded in my bag.

"Have you looked outside yet?" Mark yelled back.

"No, why?"

"No need to bother, there's nothing to see," he answered.

"What does that mean?" I asked, now sitting up with only my head poking out of my down cocoon.

He said the one word none of us wanted to hear on this trip. "Whiteout."

My nose and chin were already uncomfortably cold, but I had to see if it was true. I freed my arms, unzipped the soaked and frigid tent flap and rain fly and stuck my head out into the cloud.

"Shit!"

I could see Mark's tent, maybe 30 feet away, and the water a few steps beyond that, and then nothing but white. We could have been inside a giant ping pong ball for all we knew.

"Might as well hunker down," Mark called out. "We're not going anywhere for a while."

Even with a GPS, navigating in a whiteout was not only dangerous, it was impossible. A GPS can tell you exactly where you are, but you can't get to where you want to be if you can't see where you're going. You're doomed to walk in circles, a talent we'd previously demonstrated even under the clearest of conditions. He's right, I thought, and zipped back into my warm little cocoon.

I have a small tent. Someone once referred to it as a nylon coffin. As with most activities, there are conflicting philosophies in backpacking. One school of thought to which I fully subscribe is "the lighter your load, the farther you'll go." The corollary to this is "pack light, freeze at night," to which I also fully subscribe. My tent is merely a place to sleep; it is not a place to lounge around.

The moniker "nylon coffin" is not entirely inaccurate. While it does provide excellent protection from most of the elements, it limits my range of activities to the following: (a) lying on my back with my arms by my sides, and (b) sitting up with my arms by my sides. It is by no means the best place to while away the hours waiting for a dense fog to lift. So it was with great relief that I finally heard Mark call out that it was time to get moving.

Katie was the first to answer. "I don't know, it's still pretty thick."

"Let's at least try," Mark said. "If we only get a short distance and can't see to navigate, we can always come back here, or just hunker down again. Tell ya what," he added. "I'll even make us some coffee."

Apparently the promise of a warm beverage is all it takes to convince Katie and me to risk our lives, because we were immediately out of our tents and packing. Which was extremely difficult—the wind was increasing and every piece of gear was drenched from the previous night's rain, which had slowed now to a mist. No matter how much we flapped our tents, they were quickly wet again. My fingers became numb from handling the wet, chilly gear. I reluctantly stuffed my feet into soaked boots and put my final pair of dry socks on my hands; I hadn't packed proper gloves.

Wrestling against the wind to break down my tent and stuffing the remainder of the gear into my pack was especially cumbersome without thumbs, but I ultimately succeeded. Mark arrived with a hot cup of instant coffee. "Nice gloves," he said when I reached for it. "What brand are they?"

"Darn Tough," I told him, and thanked him again as Katie joined us to look at the map. "OK. Now. Where the hell are we going?"

■ ■ ■

First we had to cross the creek. At the wide point near the campsite, a smattering of rocks provided perches upon which it might be possible, were one to possess superior agility, to cross via a series of hops and still remain dry. None of us felt we possessed the requisite level of agility. Downstream the creek appeared to narrow enough that it might be possible to leap across. Upon closer scrutiny, it became obvious that the crossing would indeed be narrower, but that the water was gaining energy and speed as it was channeled into the gap. There it looked pretty deep.

Cresting the ridge at precisely the point we were

hoping to eventually reach was a lone caribou headed our way. Mark leaned in to whisper to us. "If we'd been just a bit earlier, we would have met him right there on the trail."

"He's looking for a way to cross," Katie said. "Let's see what he does."

Either it didn't see us, or didn't care. The caribou scanned left and then right before gingerly placing a hoof into the creek. The water didn't look too deep or fast where he was, and I was optimistic for it, and us. "If he can wade across there, surely we can too." At precisely that moment, the caribou lost his balance and fell in, plunging up to his neck. The formerly majestic beast actually looked embarrassed now as it clambered and scrambled back up onto the rocks. He shook his head vigorously, snuffed, and jumped back in, swimming to the far shore. Seemingly unaffected by his sudden bath, he galloped along the stones, and up and over another ridge far to our right, vanishing into the mist.

"Yeah, let's try our luck back at the wide spot."

We retreated and Mark led the crossing. I followed, and Katie wisely waited on the shore, waiting until we found a successful path. The creek was littered with rocks, and we hopped from one to another, finally finding ourselves standing in a spot where the next safe step was just slightly farther than either of us felt comfortable attempting.

"You know what, Mark?" I said. "My feet have been soaked all day, every day, and I'm sure they will be all day today. I don't know why I'm even bothering to try anymore." With that, I jumped off my rock, into knee-deep frigid water and splashed my way to the other side, still at least wearing dry socks on my hands.

Katie removed her boots and socks, put on her river shoes, rolled up her pants and followed. Mark was able to make the leap after all. He continued to carefully pick and choose his steps, and soon enough the three of us were across. An hour later, having traveled only a quarter of a mile, we realized we'd forgotten to eat breakfast.

■ ■ ■

The fog was starting to thin out, but it was by no means clear. Fortunately, we'd reached an area where the terrain consisted of many relatively small ridges and valleys. Visibility was low, but each horizon would now be near enough to coexist inside the ping pong ball with us.

For another hour we climbed more ridges and descended more valleys. At one point we threaded the needle between two ponds along a strip of dirt as the wind whipped the water into a fury and the waves lapped at us like an incoming tide. Hunkered down in a low spot between the shores was a flock of ptarmigans seeking refuge from the wind. They flapped and chirped at us as we tried to pass without disturbing them.

Despite the constant up and down, we were gradually gaining elevation. The wind was picking up.

"At the top of this next ridge," I shouted over it, "we should be able to see Gros Morne again!"

With my next step, an invisible hand shoved me hard to my left. I stutter-stepped and planted a pole to maintain balance. It was like someone had grabbed my pack and tried to wrestle me down. I looked up and saw that Mark and Katie had been pushed as well. Mark yelled something, but over the sudden roar of the wind, and the flapping of my hood, it was incomprehensible. "WHAT?" I yelled.

"It's getting pretty windy!"

As we crested the next ridge, two things happened: We regained sight of Gros Morne, and impossibly, the wind got even worse. We gave up on talking, and had to lean pretty hard to the right to prevent being pushed over. Our packs worked like spoilers as powerful gusts used them to shove and wrench us in every direction but forward. Eventually we took a knee and huddled together, squinting and teary-eyed. Imagine sticking your head out the window of a car riding down the highway. Of course, Mark decided to shoot some more pictures.

We were impressed by his efforts. While Mark fought with his tripod, it became clear to us that the violent winds might add a certain level of danger to climbing Gros Morne. In addition to throwing us around, the wind was also making it difficult just to keep our eyes open. We resolved to go around instead of over. I was okay with that. The view from here, of the Big Lonely shrouded in clouds, seemed a fine way to remember it.

We were in sight of Ten Mile Gorge, a massive scar in the earth that led to Ten Mile Pond, a fjord similar to the one by which we'd entered. Across the gorge the opposite plateau revealed a jagged notch gouged by a waterfall that vanished into the emerald canyon below. We craned our necks to see but had no hope of ever finding its bottom. This magnificent cliff marked the terminus of our westward journey; we had no choice now but to turn left and begin to look for the descent.

The wind continued to resist us as we stumbled forward, looking for the cairn that would tell us to begin climbing down. We thought we had found it several times, only to approach the edge, peer over it, and agree that there was no way in hell anyone was going to get down that without ropes. When Mark excitedly pointed at the seven foot tall stack of rocks, we knew that was it, the cairn marking the number one toughest descent.

The drop into Ferry Gulch was similar to our crazy climb up that first waterfall days ago, but in reverse. The terrain was frighteningly steep, and much of our effort was spent scrabbling blindly for handholds and footholds, using roots like ropes, and trying not to plummet to our deaths. At least the wind died down as we lost elevation. Finally, hands and feet sore from the climb, we arrived at the bottom, where a small pond awaited with a picnic table that, after our wilderness adventure, seemed almost surreal.

Slack-jawed and panting, we sat at the table and wolfed down a handful of carbs to get us through the last five kilometers. Then, fuel intake complete, we followed the trail past Gros Morne Mountain. Finally able to walk normally again, I whistled and sang to myself, all the while marveling at how ridiculously long and fast my strides had become again. Even an hour-long clamber through the scree field at the base of the mountain couldn't spoil my mood, though Katie briefly stopped talking again.

The trail wound down and away from the mountain, through bogs furnished with luxurious wooden boardwalks again, complete with benches and colorful signs depicting the various creatures and plants we'd encountered during the previous days. The trail then took us into the trees, and in the full heat of the day I sucked the last drop of water out of my Camelbak. Another hour passed, and then, finally, there was a clear break in the trees up ahead.

A power line. A bulletin board. The glint of sun on a windshield.

The end.

I dropped my pack, sat in the gravel next to the car, and pulled off my boots. Then caught a whiff of them, and looked for the nearest dumpster.

CHAPTER 16
NORTHERN LIGHTS

Sunday March 16
North Carolina, USA

I said goodbye to Katie at the curb of Charlotte airport and watched her drive off. Inside the terminal, I immediately spotted Mark on a dark leather seat by the window. He wore the face of a man who had just stubbed his toe for the second time and had already gone through all of the fun swear words.

"We're not going to make our flight to Iceland," he said.

"Why not?"

Mark took a deep breath and pressed his lips together. "Our flight to Boston has been delayed by two hours, which leaves us seven minutes to make our connection to Iceland. And I couldn't do anything because you have the tickets."

Since the Long Range Traverse, Mark and I had done a lot together, but this was our first overseas thing as a team in a while, and it was not getting off to an auspicious start.

Our plan to fly through the night and arrive in Iceland the next morning was going to need revising. Still, a true worst case scenario would involve pirates, I reminded Mark, who was not amused.

The lady at the baggage counter couldn't help us, and the ticket lines were long so I called instead. A very nice airline phone lady picked up after the 20th commercial for their credit card. After a few minutes of clicking and typing, she told me that the best they could do was send us via Frankfurt, Germany, getting into Iceland just before dinner. We'd lose our day of downtime and free range exploring, but would still have time to make our first scheduled event, a Northern Lights tour. In fact, most of the rest of the week was a jam packed itinerary, a planned tour nearly every day. Mark's passion for photography and mine for wandering fare better without a rushed schedule.

"Have you checked any bags?" Very Nice Airline Phone Lady asked. I told her that we had, and she assured me that they would meet us at our destination. "Could you please describe your bag?"

"Sure. It's the one that has that computer-generated barcode on it that you charge so much extra for. Other than that, it's a medium-sized black rectangle. Should stand right out."

"Tell her mine's red," Mark said into my other ear.

"Okay sir, we've made a note of it. All you have to do now is go to the nearest customer service desk and show them your passport."

Mark and I spent the next hour in line. After collecting our new boarding passes, we had a quick meal neither of us finished and a beer which we definitely did.

Monday, March 17
Frankfurt, Germany

"How many times has that pink one gone around?"

"Three."

"I'm going to give it one more turn," I said. "I think they're still putting bags out."

"I'm going to go ask someone," Mark declared, and headed to the nearest uniformed person, in this case a friendly-looking employee from another airline. She told him we didn't have to get our bags here and take them through customs — they'd be waiting for us in Iceland.

She wore a smart hat. And a pin. We believed her.

Later that same Monday
Keflavík, Iceland

"How many times has that flowery one gone around?"

"Fuck."

All of our clothing and most of our cold weather gear was gone. We filled out some lost luggage forms, then went out and tossed our meager carry-on belongings into the seats of the shuttle bus.

Miles in the distance were jagged, snow-covered mountains and plateaus. The ocean surrounded us on three sides, shimmering bright blue. Squat buildings, small cars, and weird road signs filled in the foreground.

Mark flipped through our itinerary. "Once we get to the hotel, we'll have about two hours before the guide meets us. We should have plenty of time to find a place to replace some of our gear and a quick bite to eat."

We checked in and shared our woes with the concierge. She showed us on the map where the nearest outfitters were—only a few blocks away. "But you will probably not get what you need at these places," she said.

"Why not?"

"Because everything closes at six o'clock," she said. It was 6:05.

She gently took the map from me and pointed to some other spots. "You can still try, though. There might be some others, here and here."

"Thanks!" we said, and bolted for the door. "What street are we on?" I asked Mark.

"I see the sign but I have no idea," he said. "Looks like Sherfta-herm...something-voss. And a D with a line through it."

I stuffed the useless map into my pocket. "That way!" I announced, and headed towards a street that looked like it had some shops. Most were closed, but a few still had lights on. I managed to scare up a pair of merino wool long johns, Mark got what he needed, and we rushed back to the hotel with just under an hour before the van was to pick us up. At the restaurant, we split a fancy club sandwich and a gigantic bowl of French onion soup, and moments after we paid our bill, the van arrived.

. . .

We stepped outside and were greeted by Gilli, a friendly man with a round face who shook our hands and opened the van door. We squeezed into the back, behind a gregarious Australian couple we had met earlier in Frankfurt. It turned out that he was both an astronomy enthusiast like me and a photographer like Mark, so his wife mostly looked out the window while we boys conversed in the universal language of gear talk—lenses, focal lengths, apertures and so on. The sky darkened and we drove east for about an hour, stopping in a remote field.

"Okay, now let's talk about the aurora," Gilli said as he rounded us up. "It is very unpredictable. Sometimes it is very bright. Sometimes it is very faint. And you must know that most times we see nothing at all."

While we waited, I passed around my binoculars and showed people how to find Jupiter and the Orion Nebula. After about 15 minutes of looking up and shivering, Gilli shouted, "Look to the north! Do you see it?"

There was definitely something, a dim glow at best. It could have been a cloud catching the moonlight. Mark shot a hasty 30-second exposure, then looked at the screen on his camera. "Guys, that's it! Come look!" The long exposure revealed what our eyes could not: a wispy green glow, like radioactive smoke pouring from an invisible stack.

The group formed a crescent behind him, confirmed

that the dim glow was in fact aurora, and dispersed to set up their own tripods. As they did so, the glow brightened into a neon lime wave.

For the next 30 minutes we stared up at the sky, watching the lights dance as long as we could stand the cold, then retreating to the van to warm back up. Without my boots, my feet stung from the cold. People did jumping jacks, and those with cameras danced with their exposed fingers tucked into their armpits.

We watched for another half an hour, and by then the lights were fading, we were all cold, and it was late. We piled into the van and headed west, back to town.

As we drove, frost formed on the inside of our windows, thick enough that it had to be scraped. A Korean tourist in the row ahead of us rubbed a portal into his window, pressed his forehead to the cold glass, and suddenly started hooting and pointing. "Ohhh! Ohhh! Look! Lights!"

He began making bigger and bigger circles into the frost with his glove. I leaned forward and shared his view. "HOLY SHIT!" I yelled. "You guys have got to see this! Look!"

More people began pawing at the glass and yelling, so Gilli pulled over. We bundled back up and spilled out into the cold yet again. The entire sky was ablaze with radiant plasma, as though someone had flipped a switch. Impossibly tall curtains of light swirled in massive loops overhead, bright green like weird alien searchlights. Emerald spikes appeared, shimmered and shrank, reappearing moments later half a sky away. Soft moon glow illuminated snow-covered mountains and lava fields in the foreground.

This second show continued for another half an hour, maybe more. Still cold but no longer shivering, we stood and gaped at the heavens, watching ions glow and soar above until the lights subsided. Then we climbed back into the van and rode back in silence, still in awe of what we'd seen. It was after midnight by the time we returned to the hotel. Yet sleep did not come easily, which was unfortunate because tomorrow we were going to go inside a volcano.

CHAPTER 17
FANCY PANTS

SLEEP HAD NOT come easily, and it didn't stick around once it did. After a fitful night of groggily checking the alarm clock every hour or two, at 7:30 a.m. I submitted to being red-eyed and grumpy and put yesterday's clothes back on. My only pair of socks were a bit crusty at the start of their third day, so I turned them inside out. Good as new.

Mark was already downstairs when I arrived. He looked about as rough as I felt, and confirmed he had slept about as well. The coffee was good enough to improve our mood. When the van arrived it was empty apart from the driver, Palli, who was handsome, blond, and stood about 6'5", or 6'8" with his man-bun.

As we drove to pick up the other travelers, we told him about our Northern Lights excursion the night before. When we told him our guide had been Gilli, Palli said, "Gah! We all so much hate that guy. He always sees the Lights. Every time he takes a group out, he knows just where to look. His eyes are better than anyone's should be. He sees the aurora half an hour before it's really there. He is just the best. We hate him."

Palli concentrated on the road while he said this, and only the barest hint of a smile betrayed his irony. Then he couldn't hold back a grin. "Well, good that you saw it. It was supposed to be all clouds last night. You were lucky to be with Gilli."

Our next stop was at another hotel a few blocks from ours. Here we picked up our travel companions for the day, a shy pair of young lovers from France, newlyweds it turned out. Palli opened the door for them, they said "thank you," and slid into the row behind Mark.

"Okay guys," Palli started as we left the city. "Do you see this big mountain across the water?" We couldn't possibly miss it. "She is called Esja. There are trails that go to the top. I have a friend who goes up her every day before he starts work. He does this for exercise because it is crazy. But she is beautiful up there."

"Do you call all of your mountains 'she' and 'her?'" I asked.

"No. Just the ones who are women. The man mountains are 'he.'" His expression told me that this should have been self-evident.

As we drove on, the city faded in the distance, while the road ahead vanished into the approaching snowstorm.

Palli continued, "Okay, our first stop today will be a place called Thingvellir. This is a very important place in our culture because it is where the Vikings held their parliament. And it is the place where two continental plates join. You can stand with one foot in America and one foot in Europe. It is a beautiful place."

We rode for a few minutes in silence, everyone but Palli straining to gawk at the landscape through the glass and thickening snowfall. The mountains reminded me of the fjords from Newfoundland. They sprouted at nearly 90-degree inclines, soaring straight up from the snow-covered earth, not really peaking but leveling off at 90 degrees again to form high plateaus, a kind of split-level home for ice giants.

"Guys, I want to tell you another reason why Thingvellir is such a special place." We turned our attention to Palli. It was getting hard to see anything outside anyway. "I want to tell you the saga of Egil. This guy was very powerful. He was very successful as a farmer and he had a lot of money. He was such a badass though, because much of his money also came from just killing guys and taking their stuff. Their money, their land, their women. You know. This guy was a Viking.

"So anyway, he has many children, but his oldest son, his heir, is a disappointment to him. His boy wants to look at paintings and wear silk clothes. He is what you would call in English a 'fancy pants.'

"So his badass Viking father does not want all of his life's treasure to go to this fancy boy, so he decides to do something else with it. When Egil is very old and he knows that he can probably not live much longer, he calls his slaves in secret. 'Go and pack up all of my silver,' he commands them. 'Put the trunks on your backs and start walking to Thingvellir.'

"His plan is to take all of his treasure and go to the parliament at Thingvellir while it is in session. He plans to climb to the cliffs above it and throw his silver down upon them, because it is Egil's dream to see the most powerful men in the land crawl on their hands and knees, picking up what he is throwing away.

"But Egil is so very old. And when he gets about halfway there, he realizes that he is going to die soon. So he commands his slaves to bury all of the silver. They do this and then he kills them. He dies somewhere in the fields there, and the Icelandic people believe to this day that his treasure is still buried at that place. You will see people walking all over the place with metal detectors in the summertime."

We arrived at Thingvellir and Palli walked us to the edge of an overlook. From where we stood we could see the canyon tracing a line where the tectonic plates met. A walking path led down into the canyon, and we wandered among the rocks and snow, stopping often to photograph. The sky was bright white, and snow covered nearly everything, only broken by towers of black volcanic rock. A stream so clear it looked empty ran through the center of it all.

An hour later, we were back in the van and headed for a waterfall called Gullfoss. When we arrived, I pushed open the passenger door and the wind slammed it shut. I gave the door a second try, and we all climbed out and immediately leaned into the blowing wind.

The wide Hvítá River rushes southward, and at Gullfoss it turns sharply to the west, tumbles down a three-step staircase, and then abruptly plunges 105 feet down into a long, wide crevasse. As we approached the falls, the crevasse was obscured from view, so that it appeared that a mighty river simply vanished into the earth. Towers of frozen spray made it impossible to tell where the water ended and the land began.

"Do not go into the falls," Palli said. "You will die." A thin, ankle-high rope and a shred of common sense were all that separated us from certain doom. High winds whipped freezing spray and hard bits of ice against our faces. To view the falls I resorted to turning my back completely and pointing my camera behind my head.

▪   ▪   ▪

The next place on our day's itinerary was Geysir. The natives' term for the gushing, geothermal vents found all over the island is the only Icelandic word widely adopted into other languages. Steam squirted out of tiny holes in the earth while natural jacuzzis simmered and churned. One bore a sign depicting a thermometer with a frowny face and the warning, "You will boil in this." Another ankle-high rope was all that kept us from falling in—Icelanders seem shockingly cavalier about safety. The air reeked of sulfur.

A crowd of about 100 had gathered beyond the boiling pools. They were staring intently at a large hole in the ground. We joined them.

The hole, in addition to belching steam, also had a level of greenish-blue water rising and falling at its opening. The water would get sucked below, the hole would burp, and the water would rise in a small dome and spill over the edges of the hole before getting sucked back down. With each rise and fall the height or depth increased until finally, with a loud sulfurous fart and a hefty splash, the whole thing violently sprayed dozens of feet into the air. This happened every six minutes until we had seen enough.

A second geyser at the site is even bigger, Palli told us once we were on the road again. "The bigger one hasn't erupted in years, and we think that means that the lava flow has changed. It might come back, but it probably won't. A few years ago when it was declining, the guy who owns the gift shop nearby was nervous that it would affect his sales. So it is rumored that at night he began sneaking soap into the geyser."

"Why soap?" Mark asked. "Does it have something to do with the surface tension?"

"Something like that," Palli said. "It allows the water to boil at a lower temperature, plus it makes bubbles, and I guess he thought that tourists would like to see that. Well his plan does not work, and he just wastes all of this soap. He is like some kind of bad Scooby Doo villain, you know?"

The heavy snow and wind had turned into a full-blown whiteout. The road was barely detectable as an off-white path stretching out into the pure white ahead of us. Bulbous mounds of porous black rock poked out of the snow, some the size of soccer balls, others like discarded bean bag chairs. This, for as far as the eye could see. Which in this snow was not far. But we could still make out the volcano up ahead, our final destination.

Palli stopped the van by a pile of lava rocks that looked exactly like all the other piles of lava rocks.

"We're here," he announced. He passed out helmets and headlamps and led us into the field of rocks, the volcano looming behind us.

The opening was about the size of a manhole, although nowhere near round. When Palli told us it was the entrance, we laughed, hoping it was another of his jokes. But he quickly disappeared inside it. We called after him, but whatever words he yelled back were muffled by the wind and the snowdrifts piled at the entrance. We had no choice but to follow him in.

"Since I'm smaller, I'll go first," Mark said. While I adjusted my headlamp and thought, *How's that a reason to go first?* he dangled his legs into the opening, leaned back like a kid on top of a sliding board, and vanished into the blackness. The French couple went next. I shined my lamp into the hole and saw faces looking up. Taking care not to kick snow on them, I plunged in.

Inside the cave, I smacked my hands together to get the snow out of the cheap mittens I'd bought back at Thingvellir. At least down here in the cave it was warmer, about 50 degrees, and there was no wind. Water dripped around us.

"Do you remember Gollum, from *Lord of the Rings?*" Palli asked us. "Do you remember how he walked on his hands and feet? You will have to do this in some places in this cave. And here you will have to crawl on your belly, but just for a few meters." With that, he dropped down like a Marine in mud and scampered through a crevice the rest of us hadn't noticed until we saw his headlamp fading from within.

I managed to scoot through the narrow opening

with a few inches to spare. The floor was mostly wet with slick patches, but rough and jagged in some places. In the next chamber, Palli tilted his chin up directing his headlamp onto the ceiling of the cave. "Do you know what we call these things that hang down?" Before anyone could reply 'stalactites,' he answered his own question gleefully: "Lava titties! Because they look like the things that hang from a cow."

He mimed milking, and I suggested, "Udders?"

"Titties!"

He pointed out to us that the rock walls around us were round. We were in a lava tube, left behind by magma that had last flowed through here 1,200 years ago. Palli then had us turn off our headlamps, and we were in total darkness.

"Have you heard of the hidden people?" he asked. The French couple stopped their giggling.

"Most times you hear them referred to as elves," he continued. "Many people here in Iceland take the elves very seriously. When a farmer gets a new piece of land for the first time, one of the things he will do is to check the field for elf stones. I don't know how they know which ones are the elf stones, but sometimes they find one, and when they do, they will not touch it. They believe that bad things will happen if they touch one, so they will plow their fields around them.

"They take this very seriously. But to me—I hope no one is offended by this, but it is like the Americans and their invisible man in the sky. These things are stories we tell our children, no more."

Water dripped. "Would you touch an elf stone?" I

asked.

"No! I would not touch it, and I would not let my children touch it."

Then he told us another legend, this one involving that "invisible man in the sky" whom most Icelanders tell surveyors they do not believe in.

"There was a village that found out they were going to be visited by God. So they cleaned themselves up as best as they could and put on their best clothes. But some of the children were dirty from playing and would not bathe. Because they didn't want God to think they were dirty people, they took these kids and they hid them.

"And on the day that God came to visit the village, he said, 'You have hidden your children from me. So now they will remain hidden!' And these are now the hidden people. Some people say that if you ever see one, they will take you and you will be forever hidden too. Now, where do you think the hidden people live?"

"In the lava tubes?" Mark replied.

"In the lava tubes," Palli said. "When I was a boy, seven years old, my father took me into a lava field just like the one we are under. He pointed to the hole in the ground and said, 'Boy, get in that tube.' He is my father; I had to go in. He brings me deep into the tube and we turn off our lights and he tells me this story of the hidden people. Can you imagine telling this to a 7-year-old boy! But now I have to ask you one more question. When we turn our lamps back on, would you rather there was one less of us...or one more?"

We clicked the lamps back on to find our number neither diminished nor augmented. We scuttled on to the next chamber, making sure not to hit our heads on the lava titties.

Stepping through a wide, low arch, we approached a peculiar formation hanging from the ceiling. Wax-like drips of rock hung frozen in place from what looked like an overturned bowl, and Palli showed us how to pose a photo in order to make it look like an alien was sucking out our brains.

Then we hunched, scooted, and Gollum-walked back to the place where we had entered, finally arriving at a dimly glowing white crack. Because of the heavy snow, we had to dig our way out of the cave before we could get back inside the warmth of the van.

"You have had a very big day," Palli announced. "You have seen a huge waterfall. You have seen water gush forth from the earth. You have stood in the parliament of Vikings, and crawled in a lava tube. But your visit to Iceland would not be complete without what I want to show you next."

As we drove, I became aware of a fishy smell. Within moments the odor was overpowering. About a quarter mile further on, Palli turned right, and we saw rows of wooden scaffolding marching into the distance, fading into the snow. Every available inch of space had a large fish head dangling by a string.

"That is the smell of money," Palli declared.

Salty smoked fish is a popular snack in Iceland. We had seen sacks of the stuff in many of the shops, usually on display with the chips or cookies. We continued to drive toward the stench until we were upon it. The inside of the van smelled like a Captain D's dumpster and we hadn't even opened any windows or doors yet. Deciding it couldn't get any worse, we opened the door and walked among the stinky heads.

Dead eyes and silent mouths gaped at me from every direction. "Hey, Mark," I called. "Check this out! It's an angler fish." I lifted it by its twine.

"Whoa!" Mark lifted his camera to his eye. "I didn't know they were that big."

Twice the size of a football, the thing was all head and teeth. A long, petrified dangly bit arched from the beast's forehead, with some sort of lure at the end. The wind spun the thing toward me and I flinched. "Did you get your shot? I'm putting this down."

Drying fish heads are only interesting for so long, so we climbed back into the van. When we returned to our hotel, our missing gear had finally arrived. After a shower and long-awaited change of clothes, we filled ourselves with food and beer, and sleep this time came easily.

CHAPTER 18
THE CLIFFS OF WOO

IT FELT SO GOOD to put on fresh clean pants. I looked out my window and saw gray. This told me nothing, so I headed downstairs. Mark was already seated, and I filled a small plate and joined him. We ate our breakfast in silence, taking turns staring at the gray sky and the big trucks.

In Reykjavík it seems that every other car, truck, or jeep is on stilts. Mercedes, for example, makes this thing that's basically a cross between a passenger van and a monster truck. A retractable ladder hangs from the door so that you can get above the six-foot cartoonish balloon tires and into the driver's seat, or the bridge, or whatever they call the steering area on a vessel of that size.

Moments later we were standing beside a regular passenger van, introducing ourselves to the two men who would lead us up the tongue of a glacier. Funmar looked like an '80s movie surfer dude, who we figured could direct us to the beach with the gnarliest waves in Iceland. He introduced us to his partner Thorir, who smiled and nodded.

We pulled away from the hotel and within minutes the city was behind us. It was still near-whiteout conditions, though occasionally from our side window we could see columns of steam climbing from some hidden crack in the earth. Many farms and businesses out here had built stone or cinderblock structures above these vents to harness all the power just leaking from the earth up here.

After about 45 minutes, we passed through a small town with a beautiful river and stopped at their gas station. Mark insisted on having a hot dog. Actually, this is something modern Iceland is known for. The meat is mostly lamb, they come wrapped in bacon, and you get to choose condiments in surprising colors like green and orange.

At the van, we were joined by two young women who looked to be college age, one blonde, one brunette. They were going to have to squeeze into the back row with Mark and me. They bounded into the van, giggling and omigawding. Mark and I exchanged tight-lipped smiles and carefully rearranged our gear to accommodate them.

Soon we were back on the highway known as the Ring Road because it follows the coast all the way around the island. The girl nearest Mark told the one by the window, "OmiGAWD you HAVE to tell me!"

"No, I can't. It's GROSS!" her friend replied.

"OmiGAWD you HAVE to tell me!"

This went on for some time, until Funmar turned and addressed the group. "If you look out the left, and look very far over that mountain, that peak you see in the distance—that is Eyjafjallajökull." Most of the passengers stared back at him in silence, probably because the word had taken so long to say that they weren't sure whether he was finished yet. This time more slowly, "Ay-yah-fyat-lah-YO-kut-lah is the big volcano that erupted in 2010, the one that caused all of the flights to get canceled and made people mad. That is it right there."

Another 30 minutes of driving and we turned onto a road which was really no more than a path through a minefield of cold black volcanic rocks. As the van bounced along the road, our horizon teetered in the distance. To the west stood a high plateau, green topped with steep brown rocky sides, littered at the base with boulders that had tumbled down over the ages, with thin ribbons of water flowing through deep chasms from the green edges on top. To the east stood a similar sight. Sandwiched between and directly ahead was the glacier.

We were still miles away and its size was difficult to gauge. Sólheimajökull, which means "House of the Sun Glacier," looks like an overflowing dam that was flash frozen the moment it spilled. It is a river of ice, and it is huge and old. Even from a mile away, its characteristic glacial blue was easy to see.

As soon as we stepped out of the van we were grateful that our luggage had arrived the night before. The temperature was way below freezing and a strong wind tried as hard as it could to knock us off our feet. Each gust carried tiny particulate, half ice and half volcanic sand. We moved to the side of the van where there was some respite from the gale, and the two guides showed us how to put on our harnesses and fitted us for crampons, which we slung over our axes. We had a bit of walking over a field of rocks before we reached the ice, and donning them now would bend the spikes.

Distance and scale were tricky to determine. With each step, the glacier grew larger and yet somehow remained distant. From afar the glacier appeared to be a minor challenge, a few good bounds and you'd be right to the top. Standing at the base of it, the entire world was ice.

We put on our crampons and assumed a single file. "Stay in a line," Funmar shouted over the wind. "Only step where you see ice or rock. If you must step on snow, do this first." He stabbed the earth with his ice ax. "There are crevasses everywhere, and sometimes the opening is covered with snow. If you step in one, well, that is what the waiver was for." He smiled. "But don't worry, we walk on this glacier all the time, and I know where all the crevasses are. Stay in line, only step where we step, and we will all be fine. Ready?"

"Does this ice, like, go all the way down?" one of the young ladies asked. "You know, to like, sea level?"

Funmar explained that no, we were still above solid earth, pointing back to where we had just come from. Glaciers are basically rivers of unmelted snow that has compressed into ice over time. Ahead of us, the river of ice grew to a thousand feet thick, and higher still, if we were brave enough and equipped to walk for days.

Despite the pockmarks from dozens of crampons, the ice still retained a clear, smooth quality where it showed through the drifting snow and black sand. Unlike the ice we commonly see on sidewalks and roads, beneath this ice was nothing but more ice. That much ice, even with all the sediment and boulders within, was like glass—foggy glass, but still translucent and shimmering. You could look as deep into it as any lake, only this was solid. The surface rolled before us like swells in the sea, perfectly motionless, trapped in time. There were curlers and breakers, eddies and swirls, all frozen solid around us like some vast stage set depicting an ocean. Where the sun caught the waves just so, they shone bright blue, a frozen sky beneath our spiked feet.

We crisscrossed and zigzagged up the massive frozen tongue, stopping on a curved ridge while some people adjusted their gear. Funmar asked us, "Who can guess how much snow does it take to compress into a single centimeter of glacial ice?" People in the group began shouting numbers. "How about eight meters!" he said. "What happens is, every year the snow piles up on the glacial cap north of this place. Every year the pile gets bigger and bigger, hundreds, thousands of feet high. It is a mountain of nothing but snow. And the stuff at the bottom," he clapped his hands. "Smashed! Compressed into sheets of ice by the weight of the mountain. And then after hundreds of years, just like a glass that is too full, the ice slowly spills over the edges and we get the parts like this." He pointed down. "The tongue of the glacier."

He went on to tell us about the tremendous power of the glacier, how it shapes the land and moves the mountain. If the volcano beneath the glacier were to erupt, it would instantly melt the glacier, creating a tsunami that would travel from the center of the island out to sea, taking thousands of people with it.

Up ahead and over the next ridge we came to a steep drop. Funmar produced a collapsible shovel from his pack and quickly dug a staircase into the slope before us. Once we climbed to the bottom, he showed us an ice cave with the promise of a lovely surprise inside. The cave and whatever the surprise was were small enough to only hold two or three people at a time, so we took turns. Mark with his tripod elected to go last; he and I squatted low and quickly made our way to the end of the tunnel. The terminus was not a dead end, but rather a sharp turn straight up as the tunnel became a chimney which rose about 50 feet to a tiny patch of sky. The sun shone into the chimney, causing the walls to radiate bright blue. We were out of the wind and could hear tiny water drops all around us. I wondered how long this tube had been there, and how long it would remain. Is it still there today?

We exited the tube, rejoined the group, and scaled Funmar's stairs back to the ridge. So far, Funmar had done all of the talking while Thorir scouted ahead, poking for crevasses. His long legs and slim build gave him goat-like properties as he skimmed up the ice. When I caught sight of him at the next ridge, he was scaling it vertically. Suspended from dual axes which in silhouette looked like a praying mantis claws, he kicked his toe spikes into the wall. Putting all of his weight on those, he then wrestled one ax out of the ice, reached up to chop it in higher, and repeated with the other. Kick, kick, ax, ax, up he went. In seconds he was up 60 feet, as easily as you or I would walk up the aisle at the grocery store. He squatted, dumped some things from his pack, and began hammering and screwing something into the ice. We saw him put his empty pack back on to keep it from blowing away, and then we were behind another frozen wave, making our way to the base of the wall Thorir had just scaled.

I examined the solitary cheap rental ax in my left hand, and noticed that one of my crampons had come off. I squatted to reattach it while the rest of the group continued their descent. Also, my harness had been giving me a wedgie and probably explained why my ass was becoming numb. Temporarily blinded by the sun glinting off of Funmar's perfect white smile, I hurried to catch the others.

■　■　■

Here in the shadow of the ice wall, looking up, the true slope was intimidating. The first meter or so was a walkable 45 degrees. The next 50 feet were truly vertical, with a deep crack running almost to the top. The final 15 feet jutted back out as the underside of an overhang. Thorir's silhouette crested the edge, and suddenly the sky was filled with coils of falling rope.

Funmar produced a pair of mantis claws and demonstrated the technique we had observed. Kick, kick, ax, ax. Lift with the legs, use the axes for balance. Make an A-frame with your body. Got it? He then demonstrated the most important thing: the safety rope. He handed one end to Thorir, who had rejoined our group undetected, and attached the other end to his harness. He scampered up about ten feet while Thorir pulled in the slack. "You'll never fall more than half a meter!" he exclaimed, and threw himself away from the wall. He bounced like a kid in a swing, and swung back into the wall feet first, spikes catching instantly. I blinked and Funmar already had both axes into the ice and was moving upward. "Then you just go!"

Sure. Perfectly safe. He's on the rope. His buddy's got him. I wondered what was holding the rope up on top. Whatever Thorir had been pounding into the ice up above, presumably. Perfectly safe. "I'll go first!" Mark shouted, raising his hand.

I breathed a sigh of relief. I didn't want to go last, but I also wanted to watch at least one person screw this up before I gave it a go. Watching two Vikings climb a glacial wall using axes and spiked boots was pretty impressive, but I also needed to see what not to do. "Get some good pictures, dude!" Mark reminded me before accepting the good axes from Funmar.

Mark clipped into the rope, approached the wall, looked over his shoulder and called, "Climbing!" There is a language among rock climbers, a system of well-known calls and responses designed to keep everyone involved engaged, aware, and safe. I had to learn them during Mountain Warfare school in the Marines many years ago, and this was not Mark's first time on a rope either. Whether these rules apply on ice or in Iceland I do not know, because instead of calling, "On belay!" Thorir indicated his readiness by nodding and leaning into his line, tugging Mark forward into the wall. Mark heaved an ax, kicked the wall and rose about half a meter before the ice gave way, allowing his foot to slide back down.

"WOOHOOOOO!" one of the girls screamed, raising one gloved fist into the air. "YOU CAN DO IT! WOOOOOOOOO!"

Mark looked over his shoulder at me, in total disbelief. Somehow there were now four of them. I don't know if there were more from some other van or if they were multiplying, but there were more and they were louder. Apparently they were cheerleaders because they all joined in. "WOOHOO! LOOKING GOOD! WOOOOOOO!"

I can only assume that it was a desire to escape this racket which motivated Mark to climb so quickly, because a few moments later he was about halfway up, resting on a small ledge. It was only a few inches deep, but it offered more support than a few thin spikes driven into the ice. Mark panted and shook his forearms. "I can barely move my fingers," he shouted down. "This is killing my forearms!" Funmar reminded him to use his legs more, and soon he was near the top. Only the overhang remained.

Mark bent his knees slightly to test the spikes' grip, then leaned back and swung his ax into the ice above his head. It bounced off, sending a spray of ice into his face. He grunted, and when his second swat glanced off he called, "Falling!" The line tightened, and Mark dropped a few inches. Suspended from the overhang, he bicycled until he could replant his spikes.

"WAY TO GO! ALMOST THERE! WOOOOOOOOOO!" the three remaining girls called out. One of them had wandered off to find a place to pee, a fact that I and everyone else knew because it is what she screamed to her friends as she wandered off.

Funmar shook his head and laughed. "She won't find a place to pee," he said.

"YOU CAN DOOOO IT! WOOOOO!"

Mark got a few more good whacks at the ice and had reached the point where he could get his chin over the top of the ledge. The girls cheered, and Funmar told him that was as high as any of us were going to climb today and to come back down. Mark leaned into a seated position, keeping his legs straight out so his crampons made contact with the ice wall, and used his hands and the rope to guide himself back to the ground.

"How was it?" I asked, as he struggled to unclip his harness from the rope. He had already dropped the axes and was slapping at the D-ring with no success.

"My hands," he said. "Ow!"

Funmar unhooked him and said, "Great climb!" He patted him on the shoulder and asked me if I'd like to go next.

"Sure!" I said, stepping forward. "Oh wait, I want to give Mark my camera."

I walked to where Mark was now seated. His sunglasses were in a snow drift along with one glove. He was pulling off the other with his teeth. "I can't moof my hanf," he said, spitting out the other glove. He slowly flexed and straightened his fingers and I understood that it was not cold but muscle cramps that had done him in. "My left quad started jackhammering just past that ledge," he added. "This is a lot tougher than they made it look."

I clipped in, traded my cheap ax for Funmar's climbing axes, and swung for the wall. My first whack lodged solidly at the top of my reach, right where I needed it. I added an ax and kicked my right foot against the wall. It bounced off. I kicked again and that too bounced off. I adjusted my body a few inches to the right, kicked and stuck. Okay, I thought, I think that'll hold me. One more kick and I was firmly attached to the wall, arms stretched, legs perfectly straight. This was not going to get me anywhere.

I raised one toe, then the other, and straightened my legs, ascending enough to bend my elbows. It was now time to move that first ax up and repeat the process. But I'd swung the first ax so hard that it was lodged deep in the ice. I wiggled it and tugged it, and Funmar said, "Don't pull too hard or it will hit you in the head."

"DON'T HIT YOUR HEAD! WOOOOO!"

I successfully dislodged both axes, raised them and myself high enough to begin my next round of kicking. This isn't so hard, I thought, and my spiked toe bounced off the wall. A second kick failed as well, and soon I was pummeling the wall with my foot. I eventually settled on a spot to the right and finally gained traction. A bored clapper leaned closer to her friend with the bladder problem and whispered loudly, "Leave some ice for the rest of us, omigawd!"

A small shelf about 30 feet up allowed just enough room for the side of one foot. I struggled to the ledge, but did not find the relief I needed. My arms and legs were drained. My swings were going wild, and once I almost chopped the safety rope in half. I know it really wouldn't have cut the rope; they're much stronger than that. But I imagined tumbling into an icy chasm where I would remain frozen for thousands of years until thawed out by scientists in a post-apocalyptic world I'll write about some other time.

Meanwhile, back here on the icy ledge, my fingers started responding to basic commands again. I looked at the overhang and then to Funmar. "I think I might be done," I said. Funmar told me the same thing he had told Mark at this point, to use my legs. I did, and soon I was near the overhang.

I did that thing again where I kicked the ice repeatedly, and thought I heard Mark say something like, "Snuffle Gary!" But I didn't have time for his jokes and was trying now to get my ax to stick, bashing repeatedly, sending ice chips and then chunks bouncing off my sunglasses. I let Thorir's weight on the rope hold me up a few times. My forearms were screaming, and each inch I gained came at the expense of enough ice to fill a Big Gulp.

"YOU'RE ALMOST THERE! GIVE US A WOOHOO AT THE TOP! WOOOOO!"

Just another kick or two, and finally I could see the flat top of the ridge. I gave a "WOOHOO!" from the top and then rappelled down to join Mark, who was talking to a guy from New York about various places they'd each climbed. I smiled and stretched my fingers, eventually reaching some snacks from the top of my pack.

As the cheerleaders took their turns climbing, Mark asked me if I'd heard the nickname Funmar decided to give me: "Snjóflóð Gary." It sounds like "Snuffle Gary" and is the Icelandic word for avalanche, referring to all the ice spray I had sent down onto them. Nowadays I tell people my Viking name means I can chop down half a mountain with every swing of my ax, which is pretty close to true.

CHAPTER 19
LIGHT SPEED

THE NEXT MORNING, Mark informed me he would check us out of the hotel and keep an eye on our luggage while I walked the mile or so to fetch our rental car. At first I was surprised to learn they couldn't pick us up, but then he reminded me of the company's actual name: Sad Cars.

I had to cross three highway overpasses and backtrack down concrete stairs before I eventually found them sandwiched between a fish shop and a junkyard. The office resembled a long-abandoned car dealership. Sun shone through dirty windows, hazily illuminating an empty showroom with cracked tile floors. Empty desks and chairs lined the walls; no one was negotiating the price on anything. The only other person in the room was a round-faced man in a plaid shirt, and he was happy to see me.

"You must be Mark," he said.

"Gary, actually," I answered, hoping this wasn't going to be a problem.

The round-faced man squinted at the carbon paper on his desk, shrugged, and conceded. "Okay, Gary it is."

I offered my passport as proof, but he seemed to trust me. "Sign here please," he said and handed me a clipboard.

"Do you have anything in a midsize?" I asked.

Round-faced man smiled. "Come outside. I will show you what we have."

I followed him out and learned that Sad Cars was not next to a junkyard at all. This was their lot. He showed me the two remaining vehicles that still had wheels. "This one is quite small," he said, pointing. "And I think this one does not always go in reverse so well."

I silently weighed the options and nodded, accepting our fate. "I'll take the small one," I said, circling the aging teal Toyota. "I like the hub cap."

Instead of walking around the car and noting the dings, he handed me the keys and wished me luck. His wish worked, because the engine started on the very first try. A bit on the loud side, but it would go.

When I pulled up to the hotel Mark was waiting at the curb with our gear and two cups of coffee. I popped the trunk and stepped out. His face was flat. "Was this all they had?"

"Nope. This was the upgrade." I closed the trunk on our luggage, and instead of latching it responded with a loud *doonk* and bounced right back up, almost clocking me in the chin. So I pushed the lid back down slowly, and this time I felt a satisfying clunk. A little jiggle confirmed it was latched.

Mark took shotgun and passed me my coffee. When I lifted the center console lid to find a place for it, the whole thing came out, cup holders and all. I handed the contraption and all of its dangling parts to Mark. "Can you take this?"

He tossed it into the back seat and laughed. "Wow, have you ever seen such a piece of shit car?"

"Did I ever tell you," I replied, "about the time I got stuck in Possum Junction?"

. . .

The road signs were difficult to decipher, but our mission was simple. Get out of town and hit the Ring Road, the only major highway in Iceland. We didn't need to be at the airport for two more days, so this was our time to explore.

We were sticking to the southern coast, which was full of wonders we'd so far barely skimmed. Besides, a large snowstorm coming in from the Norwegian Sea was expected to bury the northern coast under mountains of precipitation. Even the monster trucks would be advised to stay away if it hit. Best we keep down here.

The island nation is a plateau surrounded by icy waters. Traveling east along the southern shore, we were treated to a nonstop show of towering cliffs and waterfalls to our left and black sand beaches to the right. Again I was reminded of Newfoundland. Those cliffs had the same shape as the fjords, with concave lower slopes that ramped up to vertical and stayed that way for a thousand feet or so before leveling off again into waves of grass the color of sand. And just as in Newfoundland, mighty cracks spewing water from the flats above. It was the first day of spring, and the snowcapped interior lands were thawing, filling the streams and waterfalls with vigor.

As we traveled farther from the city, the towers to our left withdrew, shrinking to rolling white hills sometimes dotted with ponies. I pulled over occasionally and Mark would jog to a good vantage point and then kneel at his tripod, shivering in his bright red coat, the lone spot of color in a world of white.

Our destination was the seaside town of Vík, population 300, still an hour away. We continued east and the edge of the plateau returned, gradually but then aggressively pressing us closer and closer to the sea. We rounded a point and the beach opened before us, an expansive cove miles wide. We parked again and wandered, leaning into the wind.

Smooth black pebbles stretched as far as we could see, their granularity diminishing to nearly powder at the tide line, where they were battered even finer by the thundering surf. This was a brand new beach, created by recent volcanic activity from Eyjafjallajökull, the big one that disrupted flights across Europe in 2010. The lava had created miles of coastline. Basalt molten deep within the earth had erupted, poured into the sea, where it settled into steaming piles to be ground into specks.

That freezing barrage battering the rocks had the force of a planet behind it; these currents originated on the other end of the globe starting off the shores of Antarctica. The southern coast of Iceland can be reached from there in a direct path, unobstructed by any land.

We felt less like tourists now because we could stop wherever we pleased and be uninhibited with our gawking since there was no one here to see us. It took us the better part of a day to drive a distance we could have covered in two hours nonstop. We called it the Drive of Wonder, because we wondered how many times we could see something else incredible before it became mundane. Did the locals feel that way? Was I neglecting my own sense of amazement back home, casually walking by world-class beauty but demoting it to merely part of the background?

On the side road into Vík we saw a colossal rock peninsula nearly a quarter mile long. Not a pile of rocks—a single piece as big as the Sears Tower lying on its side. The sea had eroded an arch through it tall enough for a cargo ship to pass through, had the channel not been filled with churning currents and broken off chunks of basalt.

A bit further ahead we saw the sea stacks called Reynisdrangar, craggy bent towers of rock protruding from the sea. Icelandic legend claims they were a group of trolls who were caught at sunrise and subsequently turned to stone. Mark pointed and promised to get us closer.

Vík felt vacant, and not just the hotel. We had reservations at the only place in town, and we were the only ones booked. After depositing our things in the room, I helped Mark carry tripods and lenses to the beach for a better look at Reynisdrangar.

The snow had a hard frosty crust a few inches thick. We mostly stayed on top of it, crunching our way toward the black pebbles ahead, sometimes breaking through and briefly becoming stuck up to our shins.

Mark and I climbed up onto some breakers and squinted into the gritty breeze.

Silhouetted against a red and purple sky, the spooky shadows of ghostly fingers clawed out of the frothing waves. Towering black tentacles of rough rock nearly 200 feet tall jutted from the water, seeming to grab at the gulls hovering in the wind above like kayakers surfing a wave.

To our east, far off cliffs took their own icy beating from the sea, lit against the backdrop of soft pink clouds heavy with snow. The clouds were stacking higher and higher, flattening out at the top like cotton candy anvils made of menace and fluff. Most likely one of the bands from the approaching storm.

■ ■ ■

In the morning we headed toward the storm. Not into it—the threatening thunderheads were still parked far off the coast—but in that general direction.

As we walked to the car the air was crisp and my nostrils froze shut until I wiggled my nose a few times. Again, we lazily explored the southern coast, driving east along the Ring Road.

We may have finally reached our limit, I thought. Fully saturated with wonder, we barely noticed the gargantuan ice cliffs and raging waves as we talked about home. Mark asked what was next.

"You mean as in next year, or next week?" Oh look, I thought. Another amazing waterfall.

"Take your pick," he shrugged as we whizzed past

another steam vent.

"This is the last big thing I'm doing for a while," I said, gesturing indifferently toward the snow-covered lava fields around us. "I'm having knee surgery a few days after we get home." It was just an arthroscopic touch-up, an outpatient procedure. But it was also my third, and I knew to expect a few weeks of ginger limping. "But next year…"

Now I gestured with a bit more enthusiasm, this time toward some wild ponies grazing on a hill. "Next year I think I'm finally going to catch Theo!"

"Theo of 'ze highway?'" Mark asked.

"Ah yes," I answered. "Ze AT! It is a nice, how you say, beginner hike!"

Ever since Newfoundland, Mark and I had taken turns planning our next big adventures, each one wilder than the last. The one idea I couldn't get him on board with was the Appalachian Trail. Which, as it had been explained to me, required about six months. Beginner hike, my foot.

Mark whistled. "Finally going to do it, huh? I wish I could do it with you, man, but I think I'd miss Sue too much and bail on you early. No offense."

None was taken. Katie had already told me I would be on my own too. She and Mark had both offered to meet me at various spots along the trail, but that was it. I wasn't worried about loneliness though. From what I had read, hikers on the AT are never truly alone. I wondered who I'd meet.

Somewhere between Peru and Newfoundland I lucked my way out of fixing computers and into a successful but small startup company. It had fueled these jaunts with Katie and Mark, with some left over for a modest savings account with "AT" written all over it.

"Next year," I said. "No more 'someday.'"

"There are hikers out there right now, you know," Mark said. "This is prime starting season for northbounders."

"All the more reason to wait," I said. "Isn't that the same reason we're going... What's this place called?"

He unfolded the map, studied it for a second and said, "Skaftafell."

"Bless you."

Unfazed, Mark pressed on. "What about later in the month? People even used to start as late as May back in the day."

He almost had me convinced. "I'd really have to hustle to get up north before the snow, though." Then I put the idea away, for a while at least. "None of that matters anyhow, since I have to fix this knee first." I reminded him of this while yawning at another volcanic beach so fresh it was newer than our car.

▪ ▪ ▪

Perhaps I had aggravated it during the ice climb, or maybe it was mad because I spoke ill of it in the car. Either way, my knee ached with unusual intensity the whole afternoon Mark and I spent up on the flats, marveling at glaciers from above. Skaftafell is at the watery edge where ice meets sea. The ancient glacier flows for miles from its source before it breaks off into massive bergs at the same rate it grows many miles upstream, forever tumbling into the ocean in the slowest of slow motion. Far off beyond this scene, sunbeams bathed an approaching wall of imposing clouds. We could see their dark underbellies, and lighting flashed. This was as far as we would go.

We hiked back to the car and rewound the day's journey, shrugging at the wonders we'd previously yawned at, while yawning at the ones that had made us shrug. Every bit of it was breathtaking, but we were running out of steam, wondering where the wonder went.

Again, we were the only two in the restaurant back at Vík. While we ate fish and drank beer our host told us we had been wise to leave Skaftafell when we had. The whole national park now was snowed under, and no one was getting out for at least a week. Assuming one had supplies, I ventured, that might be interesting. Maybe even fun.

Mark raised his eyebrows, chugged the rest of his beer, and suggested we go to bed immediately. "We'll need to get up pretty early to make it to the airport ahead of the storm."

"Nah," I said. "The plane's not leaving early too, so we'd just be stuck at the airport instead. I'd rather be stuck here. Look, they seem to be equipped for it." I pointed to the fish.

Mark, unimpressed with my argument, frowned.

"Okay, you're right," I conceded. "You'll be up all night worrying anyway, so let's just plan to sleep on the plane. Let me finish eating and I'll get the next round.

Deal?"

He was still frowning, but not as hard. "Okay, deal. But just one more."

After just three more, we were both back to smiling.

■ ■ ■

We departed Vík at 9:14 a.m., or 9:17 if you believe Mark's account. These three minutes are still under dispute between us, evidence that our mutual senses of awe were not the only things under strain at this point of the trip.

The reason we were 14 or 17 minutes behind our agreed-upon departure time was because the trunk wouldn't shut. After multiple attempts to bash it closed, each slam bringing fewer laughs than the last, we moved everything to the back seat, thinking we might then ask around Vík for a bungee cord. Mysteriously, the lid caught on the first try after the trunk was emptied.

Mark assessed the situation. "As long as we don't open it again, we're good."

Despite this, we were still technically ahead of schedule. The storm appeared to have stalled, and we felt confident enough to stop for one last dizzying waterfall whose spray was full of rainbows. Mark put a waterproof cover on his camera and ventured in to shoot it from beneath, while I waited in the small gravel lot.

Stretching my calves, I leaned up against old trusty rusty, making one of the car's springs groan. *Right there with you, buddy.*

I walked around it one last time to confirm the

hubcap was still in place and it was. Not that it mattered. The round-faced man had told me emphatically that all they really cared about were the tires and the windows. Shipping those to Iceland is almost cost-prohibitive. The entire vehicle can rust away, but as long as you bring intact tires and windshield back to Sad Cars, they'll return your deposit.

I was almost beginning to feel affection for the rickety blue beast. As I sat down in it once more, I felt my shoe brush against the trunk release lever and heard a muffled *thoonk* from behind.

Not now.

Even though I knew what would happen, I tried anyway. I pushed down on the lid with a reasonable amount of force and it responded with an empty *doonk* and a bounce. I pushed down gently. Nothing. No clunk. I lifted the lid high, inhaled, closed my eyes and slammed down with the force of all my weight.

DOONK!

I was prepared for its counterattack this time and had already leaned back, nearly falling. Frustrated, I let loose with three rapid-fire slams. DOONK DOONK DOONK! With each slam it bounced right back, the trunk now a taunting black mouth laughing at my feeble efforts.

I probed the latching mechanism with first my finger, then a stick, and finally my pocketknife, mostly to retrieve bits of stick. I was beginning to wonder if it were possible to drive the last hundred kilometers with the trunk open when I saw Mark rounding the bend at the base of the falls.

I pushed the trunk shut and leaned on it as he walked toward me staring at the screen on his camera.

"Dude," he said. "Check this out! There were so many rainbows!"

I craned my neck as he held the camera up to show me. "Cool," I said. "Do you have any rope?"

He looked up from the screen and raised an eyebrow. "No. Why?" I stepped away from the trunk and as it opened behind me, he melted into a posture that brought back memories of canceled flights and lost luggage. "I wondered what all that banging was."

We spent the remainder of our "no hurry" time trying and failing to solve this unexpected puzzle, applying everything from force to finesse. Mark examined the latch while I wiggled the release switch, but nothing was moving. When I suggested that Mark ride in the trunk while holding it shut, he showed me his lost luggage face again.

Without warning, my senior drill instructor appeared in my mind's eye and demanded I fix this. I requested permission to venture into the tree line in order to secure a field-expedient means of securing my trunk, sir—which meant running into a nearby meadow in search of tall grass to braid into a rope. Mark grabbed my arm and pointed at my waist. "Your belt!" he exclaimed.

He was already pulling off his when I realized his plan. Folding down the back seat revealed a sturdy piece of metal we could tie to, but it was too far for one belt. Now that we had a solution, Mark's demeanor changed into an excited teacher. He showed me which knot he used to connect the two and why, which knot held the trunk, how to tighten it—all carryovers from his climbing days.

We hopped back in, started it up and backed out of our spot. The lid only bounced a little, and the steady cold air coming in wasn't too bad. It might actually hold. I checked the time, and realized we might miss our flight.

And so what if we did, I thought. I kept quiet, but unlike Mark or most people, I like a little chaos. I don't exactly go looking for it—you can't; it's chaos—but when it shows up it centers me. The whole universe and all of its daily woes vanish, and what remains is this puzzle, a thing to be solved.

My mom always told me to consider the worst thing that could happen and figure out how I would deal with that. Saying that out loud now would definitely make matters worse.

Instead, I visualized making a left out of the lot and driving away from the airport, grinning at Mark and slapping his hands away as he grabbed for the wheel. We'll get new flights, I thought. Our original tickets would probably be canceled anyway due to the storm we were now racing toward, the blizzard to end all blizzards. Cliffs and glaciers vanished in the whiteout like fog evaporating from a mirror. I stomped on the gas and the engine whined as we soared over a collapsed bridge, smashing into a snowbank on the other side, *Dukes of Hazzard*-style.

In real life, I signaled, checked my mirrors, and turned right.

Mark said nothing, but appeared calm. We were both totally quiet for the first time in days. In my head I was doing math. Here's what time our flight is, subtract an hour for security, another to get from the car place to the airport…I toed the accelerator, gently as not to appear nervous and incite a panic.

"We've got plenty of time," I said in a carefully casual tone, doubling down. "We're fine."

When we passed the next sign for Keflavík airport, it was a hundred kilometers away. To my horror I realized I'd mistakenly based my mental math on Reykjavík, which was closer. Recrunching my numbers, I saw our new necessary minimum speed was 20 kilometers per hour faster still. We were already above the posted limit, and the road had begun to swirl with wisps of flaky snow.

I toed the accelerator again, this time abandoning subtlety. Mark, who had been slouching and happily staring out the window, sat up straight and gave me a puzzled look.

"Let's see what this baby can do," I said. "Tires and glass, right?"

He turned and listened at the back seat. "The rumbling has stopped. Must've hit the sweet spot for aerodynamics and the lid's getting the spoiler effect."

I sped up more. The little wisps of snow had become tiny tornadoes, little dust devils made of diamonds spinning around us.

I compared the clock to the speedometer. Still not enough. My foot was on the floor now, every ounce of my leg behind it, calf flexed and straining to push the pedal right through the bottom of this teal shuddering rust bucket. Trembling beads of water snaked their way up the windshield as the car somehow accelerated further still.

We were in the far left lane, passing other cars like they were parked. The front end of the storm had caught us and now we were speeding through real snow. The outside world had gone grayscale and Mark clutched the dashboard as we flew through the flurries. Snow seemed to come straight at us, radiating from a point directly ahead and zooming by on all sides like a field of stars.

"Buckle up," I yelled. "We're making the jump to light speed!"

Mark braced harder, laughed and yelled back. "Light speed is too slow. We have to go right to ludicrous speed!"

But this was as fast as our sad little car would go. It shook and revolted and made every sound possible to let us know it was trying as hard as it could, and in the end our rusty buddy made it. We got ahead of the storm again, made a couple wrong turns, and still pulled into the airport's Sad Cars parking lot with minutes to spare.

This time a thin kid greeted us. While we moved our things into the shuttle, I warned him that the brakes were iffy, the center console popped out, the trunk wouldn't shut, he could keep our belts, there was a smell, and that she rattled at certain speeds. He shrugged, said, "Okay," checked the boxes marked "glass" and "tires," and gave us our receipt.

The shuttle to the airport was quick and I thought I'd sleep on the plane, but I was still jazzed from the drive.

As we taxied I considered what I'd take away from my experience, but all I could think of was the rush of the commute in the little car that could.

Tires and glass. The part that makes you go and the part that lets you see. Go and see. As a traveler or even just in life, what more could you need? A comfy seat and shiny paint job are nice, but as long as you have those first two things, you're golden. Maybe there was a little sad car in each of us. Or maybe it was just me and I was tired after all.

I closed my eyes and sighed, enjoying the first moment of real calm in days, blissfully unaware that life, as it has a way of doing, really was about to make the jump to light speed.

CHAPTER 20
SHAKEDOWN

AFTER MACHU PICCHU, I switched to a career that fed my love for exploring, a growing startup company. I wasn't one of the owners or a member of the board or anything like that, but part of their field crew. I was a traveling consultant, someone who could teach our customers how to use the software that their Fortune 500 bosses had just spent millions to acquire.

My humble slice of the pie was an expense account, hotel points, and two full closets, one lined with tailored shirts, the other spilling onto the floor, a platoon's worth of tents, sleeping bags, and backpacks. While my new coworkers were filling their garages with luxury sedans, Katie and I jammed ours full of hiking gear. The shelves were organized with water filters, bug nets, old compasses, air mattresses, trekking poles, boxes of maps, socks and gloves for any imaginable temperature, carefully labeled crates of dehydrated meals, and for some reason one brightly colored stunt kite.

The company headquarters was in Indianapolis, but we didn't have to move there. In fact, thanks to the amount of travel the job required, they told me that as long as we were close to an airport we could live wherever we pleased.

As much as we loved Savannah, the fact that we left it every weekend was an indicator that perhaps it was time to break camp. For years, Katie and I had been driving up to North Carolina to paddle and hike with Psychic Midget and the gang. So by the time I received my first assignment, we had already set stakes on a patch of dirt with a view of Mount Pisgah, one of the highest peaks near Asheville.

In retrospect I now see that relocating did more to fuel my wanderlust than to relieve it. The new job kept me in far off lands during the week, while I spent my weekends stomping around a mountainous paradise with my wife. It was permanent vacation.

Our clients loved us and the accounts got bigger and farther away. During my off hours, often in time zones that prevented calling home, I'd wander the streets or drive the roads, almost achieving the same meditative bliss that comes from hiking a new trail. Almost.

At company gatherings we'd all put on cufflinks and go on about how annoying it is to not get that first class upgrade, or when the rental car doesn't have enough USB ports. I'd play along and recount with nostalgia the sad little car with the fussy trunk I rented once.

. . .

Sometime between Newfoundland and Iceland I was offered my first international assignment, and before they even told me the country I said yes. It was India.

They confessed that they felt bad for asking me to go on such short notice, as it was an assignment turned down by a few already. No one was interested in a grueling flight followed by a week in what my bosses admitted was one of the most disease-ridden places on Earth. They warned of power outages, sweltering heat, torrential rain, and flies. This was right up my alley.

One of the connecting flights left me stranded in Bangalore for a night. Rather than find a hotel, I was content to huddle on the terminal floor behind some chairs, wrapped in my old Marine issue poncho liner. When I reached my hotel in Hyderabad, it was a golden oasis behind razor wire intended to keep the unimaginable squalor at bay. But my students were geniuses stuck with aging tech. Their hospitality was unparalleled, and when the power went out we ate chocolates and drew on chalkboards. One evening after work I saw my first non-zoo camel. It was one of my favorite jobs ever.

Back home when I excitedly shared these adventures with the other consultants they agreed that I should be the go-to guy for all their weird one-offs. I kept my passport current and they kept it full of stamps. India became a regular client, as did Australia, London, and Prague. Sure, there were still assignments like Elizabethtown, Kentucky, but our reach was expanding.

Prague was especially lovely, at least the parts I remember. One chilly evening as I strolled among the spires, I came upon a fellow tourist who seemed to be having a hard time with his map, so I stopped to help him with directions. His partner emerged from the inky shadows and conked me on the head, a mystery I was only able to piece together after waking up on the subway some hours later with an empty wallet and missing a shoe.

I must have wandered aboard in a daze. Coming to in a backwards-facing seat, I moved to the opposite side so at least it felt like I was going somewhere instead of being dragged away. When I eventually returned to the hotel, my concierge offered ice and sympathy. Katie was relieved to hear I was okay. I wrote the whole thing off as yet another occurrence of me stumbling home at sunup with a headache, limited memory of the prior evening, and zero cash.

Still, any time something unexpected came my way, I almost always had the ability to declare, "I've had worse," and mean it. The look of fear in a sys-admin's eyes when the routers spit sparks is nothing compared to the thrill of chasing down a runaway map in the wind.

It seemed there was nothing they could throw at me to dampen this never-ending positive mood swing I was riding. We were on top of the world and getting bigger, eventually attracting the attention of a much larger competitor who bought us and ruined it all.

. . .

There were just over 100 of us when we started; the whale that swallowed our school had its own zip code. We used to make our clients happy, now we made money. The bottom line was the only line. My name was on a spreadsheet of phone numbers that my new manager haphazardly stumbled through as part of our welcome aboard package. Her call came late, she addressed me as Greg, and she cut our session short, citing the six more names she needed to cross off her list before dinner.

It got worse. They cut the travel budget.

I stopped looking forward to each day and began waking from nightmares about smashing office spaces with trekking poles. My dream world colleagues dove for cover as flower pots exploded, showering useless mountains of files with precious dirt.

I had to get out.

When Mark came to me with the idea of touring a new country I said yes before he even told me it was Iceland. When we came home, I used my fancy new corporate health insurance to fix my knee, and the recovery time to ponder whether it was all worth it.

Two days after the surgery I found myself on a stump in the yard with the sun on my face. Mount Pisgah was just beginning to turn green at the bottom. It was late April. Almost time to hike, I thought, as if it weren't always that time for me.

And there it was again. A faint whisper from the woods, calling. I still needed more. I wanted something that combined the sweeping vistas of all those tours and vacations with the self-reliance I learned back in the Corps. My favorite parts of Iceland had been losing our luggage and almost putting Mark in the trunk. I'm sure there were more Marks in trunks somewhere out there, ridiculous adventures hiding in unlikely spots. But where to look?

Katie had been well aware of my growing unease. She knew I had been brushing up my resume but also that I didn't have any place in mind to send it. Maybe we could figuratively—or hell, literally—wash dishes for a while, globetrot for a bit, land somewhere fresh, and repeat.

We were still "recently young," as I had begun joking at work. At the very least we could still claim to be healthy for our age. I mean, look at how well Katie's ankle was holding up. She'd broken that thing way back in college. Which wasn't...*that* long ago. And behold how quickly I was recovering from, what was this now, my—I counted. My third knee surgery. Why, I only *kind of* need this cane, I told myself.

Now faced with my growing dossier of broken bones, surgeries, stitches, and other ailments relating to decline, my longing to sleep outside for extended periods had taken on a new sense of urgency. Minor things were taking noticeably longer to heal now. Back in our paddling days, I had once walked off a hairline ankle fracture, never discovering it until an unrelated X-ray years later. By contrast, today my neck still ached from sleeping funny a week ago.

Maybe someday was now. Either that or I'd already missed it.

I was still looking forward to the Appalachian Trail, but it wasn't supposed to appear on my radar until next year at the earliest. Katie wasn't interested in that one. Two weeks outdoors is her max.

I crossed my legs, something I couldn't easily do a

week ago. Pisgah was in full view. I knew there weren't any shelters on the trail up there, but even so I imagined one. I pictured myself on that high sunny ridge, comfortably hitting my stride in the middle of the day, with nothing on the schedule but walking. Perhaps I had eaten breakfast at a shelter, and was now trying to reach the next one by lunch. I wondered where it was and who would be in it.

A butterfly made a quick touch-and-go on my shoe. If I remembered correctly, rhododendrons would be blooming soon. They make the trail look so pretty.

This is dangerous territory, I thought, and counted in my head. *May, June, July…*

I watched my hand lift itself and extend three fingers. *August, September.* My whole hand had opened and I was reading my own palm, my future.

Could I really hike the Appalachian Trail in five months? I knew that people had done it in fewer, and if my knee or something else slowed me down, I could always find a way up north before the weather got bad and hike back, maybe even all the way home. My savings account wasn't *quite* there, but I could make a few—okay, a lot of budget cuts, cover more miles per day. I re-crossed my legs and winced. The incisions were acting up again.

There was no way I'd get the time off from work. That was fine with me. I was sure I could find something similar when I got back. And if not, I'd found jobs everywhere from kitchens to skyscrapers this far, so I wasn't worried. If I were extra frugal, I might even have time to start working on a book about it too, yet another secret someday thing.

I stood slowly and my back creaked. I had ditched my crutches the day before and already barely needed a cane. This was going fast. I squinted up toward Pisgah again and saw that tiny imaginary me, trying to find his home for the night.

Wow, I thought. This is right on the border of doable and dumb. I should go for a walk.

I settled for a quick once around the block, which out here means roughly half a mile through cow country. With the cane and some pain meds I bet I could do it in under an hour, I thought. I could feel the meds making my eyes go red, so I stopped by the house for sunglasses. The chance of running into someone was slim, but I didn't want to frighten them if I did.

By the time I made it to the big cow pasture I was feeling pretty good, shuffling right along, hardly putting weight on the cane at all, even taking a few steps without it. One of the cows was eyeballing me and I crossed the road to moo hello. She mooed back and I moved on, still thinking about my dilemma. It was job versus trail now, and the combined symphony of the stream and the birds was not helping the job make its case.

I followed a gravel road beside the stream for a while and was glad to have the sunglasses when I encountered a silver-haired lady pulling weeds from her flower garden. She was wearing sunglasses too, oversized shades from the eye doctor, which I learned about after we spent 20 minutes tallying our respective ailments, all prompted by my gnarled laurel cane and draggy foot.

When I told her I was only two days post knee

surgery she raised a hand to her throat and exclaimed, "Oh my!" She then added, as if she were reading my mind, "Well, it's good you're back up and around so quickly. Keep walking. Once you stop you're done for."

With that sage advice, she returned to her flowers.

The last road, mine, was right there. I could see it.

Work versus trail. For the past few months I had been gaining weight, drinking too much, not sleeping. Aside from weekend hikes, the only exercise I was getting was on treadmills wedged into the basements of fancy hotels. Even at the places with chandeliers in the elevators, you're still just a rat in a cage when it comes to cardio. No wonder I was falling apart. If I stuck to the plan and waited until next year to hike the AT, I might actually go mad.

I turned a corner and could see home again. Not too far now, I thought, and rubbed my thigh. Having freshly recounted my medical history for the second time in an hour, I started to realize that someday was now or never. Someday is *always* now or never.

Now.

By the time I wobbled up the front steps to the house, my mind was made up. I had used that last long straight stretch to putter along and meditate on my present situation. As I walked, every work-related thought seemed to end in analogies involving hamster wheels, while my head and eyes kept looking over my shoulder, back toward the mountain. I knew where I needed to be.

It was time to get started.

∎ ∎ ∎

One week after quitting my job I was busier than I'd been in years. I was practically leaping out of bed hours before sunrise, thrilled to take on my self-imposed chores. There was still much more to do and time was short. It was already May, far later than most northbounders begin. My knee was improving rapidly, but I hadn't tested it or my new gear yet. The AT would be unlike anything I'd ever done, in that it wasn't a camping trip—it was a *hike*.

I trimmed my gear down to what I believed to be the absolute basics, then planned what AT hikers refer to as a "shakedown hike," a quick overnighter to learn whether I'd missed anything or brought too much. With three days left to go, I hiked up to a high meadow Katie and I know well. It was a clear, starry night, and my knee and my gear performed flawlessly. The following morning I awoke to learn that all of my food had been ransacked by a bear.

I replaced my food bags and wasted the penultimate day pacing around the house like a madman. Mark came over that night, stayed in the spare room, and rode with us to Springer Mountain the following morning.

The drive takes about three or four hours, and ends on an old forest service road riddled with ruts and bumps. Even though it was sprinkling outside, the inside was awash with laughter and stories, mostly from Mark and Katie. They were exchanging private jokes from our previous trips while I stayed quiet, trying to avoid bottoming out in the deep puddles. The drizzle gradually became a downpour, a perfect start to the Appalachian Trail.

This was the most I'd sat still since that stump in the sun. Not even two weeks had passed, but it seemed like months, especially given how much Katie had done. And she wasn't even coming along on this hike.

That's when it really hit me hard. *She wasn't coming along on this hike.* I faked a sniff to brush my cheek. Things had been so crazy these past few days I didn't have time to think about missing her. It wasn't something I was used to. I was never gone for long, or she was always with me.

Katie had spent the past fortnight running around like a crazy person almost as much as I had, and for something that wasn't even her idea. Why? I didn't deserve this. All I knew was that I'd gladly hitch a ride in a thousand more cornfields to see her again for only a minute, and maybe that lump in my throat was what it felt like to be on the receiving end of that. Love.

I was really going to miss her.

She was crying too, but with laughter. Mark was making up a sea chanty about Captain Dildo and drumming on the seatback. Watching him make her smile so easily reminded me we'd be okay. For now, and most likely for later, because we had each other.

There's another age old AT axiom: *It's about the people.* I liked the sound of that, though I was convinced there was no way I was going to meet hiking companions like these two ever again.

We splashed through another bump and Mark and Katie pointed in unison. "Look! I think we're here!"

THE ADVENTURE CONTINUES...

in *Where's the Next Shelter?*

Available at Amazon in
paperback, ebook and audiobook.

ACKNOWLEDGEMENTS

This book exists because of a simple game our mom played with us when my brother and I were little. It was called "Busy Day" and the goal was simple: describe your day in the form of a story. That was it. The important part was that she listened. She paid attention and asked questions to keep us engaged. I'm still playing this game as a grownup now, walking around with my ears and eyes wide open, soaking it all in, waiting for a chance to tell anyone who will listen. Thanks, Mom.

Of course, none of this would be possible without Katie Farrar. She is my trail boss, my favorite hiking partner and the one person I'm happiest to see when I finally stumble into the glow of the fire.

Thank you, Mark Calcagni, not only for the incredible cover art and illustrations, but also for inspiring Katie and me to push ourselves and to keep exploring. P.S. We left Vík at 9:14.

I am especially grateful to have Mark Houser (aka Cornball Train) not only as an editor, but as a chum. We've been going on walks and telling stories since we were kids. Here's hoping the tradition lasts.

This project was made possible in part with help from Kickstarter. A big thank you to those supporters: Joe and Kirstin Melchionda, Daniel and Deidre Pitts, Rebecca and Gary Farrar, Gabriel Burkhardt, Mark Calcagni, Priscilla Farrar, Sacha Greer, Lisa and Sam Hutcheson, Travis Michaels, Sara Fields, Ron Fuss, Mary and Adam George, Doreen Hoover, Mark Houser, Ronnie Hull, Bill King, Mark Lesses, and Daniel Rubin.

ABOUT THE AUTHOR

Gary Sizer was born in New Castle, Pa. Years of military service and software consulting fed his passion for travel, which he now enjoys full time. After walking the Appalachian Trail in 2014, his before and after pictures went viral, and since then millions of people have seen him in his underpants. Now Gary hikes and lives in the hills near Asheville, N.C., where he occasionally records stories for NPR's *The Moth*.

FOR MORE INFORMATION

Contact Gary Sizer at TheNextShelter@gmail.com

To see photos from these and other stories,
plus original blog posts, visit GarySizer.com

Read Gary Sizer's guest blog posts, stay up to date
on hiking news, and prepare for your own
long distance hike at TheTrek.co

See incredible photos, original art, and stories
from Mark Calcagni (aka Laughing Totem)
at RaptJournal.com

Learn more about and support the Appalachian Trail
at AppalachianTrail.org

Learn about Leave No Trace principles at LNT.org

PRAISE FOR *WHERE'S THE NEXT SHELTER?*

"…easily one of the best books in the genre."
– 5-Star Amazon Review

"…the journey of Gary 'Green Giant' Sizer through the ups-and-downs of an Appalachian Trail thru-hike—literal and figurative—is fantastically chronicled in what can best be described as a 'laugh-a-minute philosophical travelogue.'"
– Jordan Bowman, *Appalachian Trials/The Trek*

"How refreshing. Sizer tells us like it is—the good, the bad and the ugly and does it with dignity and an acute sense of humor."
– D. Blankenship, *Amazon Hall of Fame*

"Visceral… my favorite book on this well-explored subject."
– Allison Tyler, *OffTheShelf (Simon & Schuster)*

Where's the Next Shelter?
Paperback and ebook available at Amazon
Audiobook available on Audible and iTunes

Printed in Great Britain
by Amazon